FOR CRYING OUT LOUD!

A LOOK ON THE LIGHTER SIDE

By

Kathy M.

ISBN: 1-4107-1777-1 (e-book)
ISBN: 1-4107-1776-3 (Paperback)

This book is printed on acid free paper.

1stBooks - rev. 11/13/03

Dedication:

This book is dedicated to all of the people in my life who refused to give up on me. I feel so grateful for having the friends and family that I do and it is because of you that I am the person that I am today.

I also want to thank with great admiration and respect, Dr. Nancy Fung and Agnes Vrieze for all of your kindness and support. It is a fact that I would not be here if it were not for all of you.

I am grateful for all that I have, in family and friends...and like every one of you...I do my best to show them so. Thanks for loving me and always believing in me. My family: Katelinn, Tylar, Scott, Eric, Mom, Dad (A.K.A. Karl), Grandma, and of course my Grandpa...up in heaven. My friends: Robin, Karen, Neyen, Di, and Eric and many more people along the way that have supported me, not only physically but emotionally as well. Throughout my life, it has been all of my 'Support Group' that has helped me push through, even when I did not think it was possible.

I want to send my greatest love and thanks to you all for ALWAYS being my voice of reason. I love you all, ALWAYS. Xoxo Kat

INTRODUCTION

I have written this book in fore thought for those of us in this lifetime, which have been stricken with "Chronic Syndromes." Yet in after thought, this book is for ANYONE that has to deal day after day with "Chronic Pain."

First off, I have given us a title called, "Syndromites R Us!" Catchy, don't you agree? The next logical question you would be asking yourself… "What is a syndromite?" In the next paragraphs, you will find out…so come and read with me!

You know you are a syndromite when you can sleep perfectly during the day and you are stunningly awake at night.

You know you are a syndromite when you forget complete conversations that you have had with others, then later they tell you what you said and it does not even sound like you! For instance, I once told my girlfriend to call me before she came over the next time…yet weeks later I asked her why she just didn't pop in to see me…nuts, no. A syndromite…absolutely!

If you have ever bought a present for someone, hid it in a place so that you would not forget it, then for the life of you…you have no recollection of where it is, you are probably a syndromite. I remember finding a whole stack of Christmas cards addressed and ready to go…it was July! Aha, you're thinking, well at least I had them for the next year…wrong, I forgot where I had put them.

If you have pain in your arm, and then suddenly it disappears, only to return to your leg, you may be a syndromite. I call these particular pains the bow and arrows, since they shoot through your body in sharp blows, at any given time.

If you could have more initials behind your name than a doctor, you are without a doubt, a syndromite. For example, I suffer from Chronic Fatigue Immune Deficiency Syndrome, Fibromyalgia, Myofascial Pain Syndrome, Irritable Bowel Syndrome, Irritable Bladder Syndrome and of course, Pre-Menstrual Syndrome. All of these put behind my name could make me look more knowledgeable than a brain surgeon…

KATHY FOREMAN SYNDROMITE SPECIALIST QUALIFIED IN C.F.I.D.S. & FMS & IBS & P.M.S.

A syndromite indeed, but a very qualified one, wouldn't you say?

If the word syndrome makes you want revenge, then you are a syndromite. I've thought of having my tombstone read, "The Syndromite Finally Rests." What do you think?

If you are tired of being tired, you are a syndromite. If you are sick of being sick and tired, you are most definitely a syndromite.

If you accidentally drink a caffeinated drink, and within minutes, you shake so badly that you can barely hang on to the cup, your ears are ringing, you feel as if you are ready to fly around the room, yes...you are a syndromite! If you wonder what you used to be like, you could be a syndromite. If others wonder what happened to the old you...you are a syndromite.

If you have a blood test done and hope that they find something, you are...hate to say it...a syndromite. How ridiculous is that?

If you are sick to death of being told, "Well, at least it isn't fatal," you are most likely a syndromite!

If you are sick of taking pills, and your purse, your car, your jacket and your pocket are like a drugstore, then you definitely might be a syndromite! My one cupboard, you know, where most people keep their dishes, is filled with medicine. My purse is stuffed with Tylenol, Gravol Phazyme, Pepto Bismal, Celebrex, Clonazepam, Effexor, Ibuprofen, and even vitamins! How about yours?

If you can't eat foods that you used to, than you are probably a syndromite! If you're stomach can't handle fruit or juice...yet it can handle beer and liquor...a syndromite you are.

If you are the last one up at a party, you could be a candidate as a syndromite. If you pay for that party in days of pain…without a doubt, you are a syndromite.

If waking up is an accomplishment, than you are a syndromite. If sleeping is an accomplishment, than you are a syndromite. If you feel like you are being held captive in your own body…a syndromite, you are.

If your pain changes from hour to hour, day to day…then you are a syndromite! The funniest thing that I found when I was at my disability hearing was that they wanted me to rate the severity of my symptoms. What kind of stupid question is that, since if you are a syndromite…all symptoms, when present, are severe! "What do you mean," they asked with bewildered faces. Well…dah, is all that came to my mind at that very moment! If your life consists of a bed, a couch, and the bathroom, you are a syndromite. If normal hygiene is an extreme effort for you, you may be a syndromite. If housekeeping is a thing of your past, you are a syndromite.

If making supper takes all the effort that you have, and being tired and in pain has become your career…chances are you are a syndromite!

If you have ever used alcohol to numb your physical pain, or you have woken up feeling as if you had drank a case of beer to yourself the night before, then realized you hadn't drank a drop...you must be a syndromite!

If your sense of direction is lost...even in your own house...and you feel as if your mind and body are in two different places... you are a syndromite.

If you have gone into a store, and have absolutely no idea why you are there, yes, you are a syndromite.

If you go to the doctors more than Italian's eat pasta (nothing against Italians) you could be a syndromite.

If you wake up soaking wet, as if you had just stepped out of the shower, you are a syndromite.

If you experience strange rashes accompanied with itching, that came from no where, and disappears as quickly as it came...you may be a syndromite.

If you have missed an entire day or more for no apparent reason, other than sleeping, you are without a doubt a syndromite.

If you would swear to someone that you have ghosts in your house, moving things, losing things, and hiding things, you are a syndromite!

When your throat is so sore that you prepare yourself for a cold coming on, and your glands are swollen to the size of golf balls, than you go to sleep to wake up absolutely fine...you are a syndromite!

If Kleenex has become your best friend as you hock up gobs of phlegm on a daily basis, and you have a box in every room, including your car...guess what? You are a syndromite.

If you have continual premenstrual syndrome...even if you are a man...you could very well be a syndromite.

If you can watch the same movie over and over again, and still not remember what it is about, you are a syndromite. Hey, this can be looked at as a good thing, as we can watch rerun after rerun, as if we are seeing it for the very first time...who else but a syndromite can say that!

'To allow ourselves to look at the lighter side...

Gives us a feeling that we are not here for nothing.'

.

What is it that we are here for? People with illnesses such as ours wonder, both silently and aloud? The answer is not a simple one, nor does it seem fair to even accept one on those real bad days, as we wonder then..."Why are we still here? "I will give you a plain and simple answer, one that every one of you may question, as even I have, "STRENGTH!" We all have and have had to find an enormous amount of strength from deep within our very souls! "What do you mean?" your asking me, right now, thinking...how am I strong when I feel so weak. The strength, I answer you is buried deep within each and every one of us.

It is from my knowledge and others as well, that I know with our illnesses, that we for whatever our individual reasons, had to be strong. Why?

I am going to say the unthinkable, yet the truth, that no one has said...abuse! Now you may be thinking that you are not in this category but let me tell you, you were, maybe not sexually or physically...but not all abuse is that noticeable, at least to the victim.

To understand this concept we must first realize that we have ALWAYS been strong...from our very beginnings in this life. I want you all to close your eyes for a moment, think of your past...before you were sick...about the struggles you faced, the feelings you felt, the thoughts that you had if you really think back! No, I am not a doctor, nor a psychiatrist, nor a psychologist, yet I know that somewhere in your past it is there…no matter how minor it may be, or you feel it to be at this time.

However, abuse comes in many forms, some very visible, and some barely visible. Neglect, abandonment, being in an unhealthy environment, both physically and emotionally are all forms of abuse! My father abandoned me at the age of 5. At the age of 8, I was thrown into a house with stepfather and 2 stepbrothers that told me right to my face that they hated me. To make matters worse he was an abusive person to my mother…the only support system that I had. I grew up with constant fighting, scared for my mother, scared for myself. At the age of 8, I had a construction worker, who had to be at least 50, stick his tongue down my throat, while every other worker watched, but didn't help. When I was 14 I found a boyfriend who told me he loved me, treated me like complete garbage. I had sex with him because he told me he would love me. More abuse…but all I wanted was love! When I was 15 I was literally attacked by a man around the age of 40, whom I fought and fought. Screaming, like never before, I was grateful when a neighbor heard me and finally called the cops. When I was 16 I had one of my so-called boyfriend's brother drive me home, only to feel me up. When I was 17 I had one of my stepbrother's friends coming on to me, saying he would teach me everything I needed to know in bed.

By the time I was 16, I was having uncontrollable panic attacks that literally lasted for days. When I was in my senior year of high school all my friends told me they didn't want anything more to do with me with absolutely no explanation!

When my mother finally left my stepfather, she became a nervous wreck, lonely and wanted him back! I had to call the ambulance one night as she was sure she was having a heart attack...no just panic we found out at the hospital. When I couldn't stand to see my own mother falling apart, I went to my stepfather and asked him to stop playing head games with her. I was worried about her health, I told him. He proceeded to tell me that if I stayed living with my mother...he would not be! I was the only thing standing in the way of what my mother so desperately wanted, so I moved out.

She thought that I was abandoning her, for I couldn't really tell her the truth when she was so frail, could I? I mean, if this is what she truly wanted...which believe me was a very hard thing to accept, I felt that I was standing in her way of happiness. I certainly couldn't tell her what he said for she seemed so frail back then!

I was working and making my own money…I could afford to move out, right! So, along with my mom upset with me, I had my very dear grandparents, whom I couldn't tell either, barely talking to me. It is no wonder that I became ill at the age of 18!

All I can tell you what got me through those years was my strength…my inner strength…for what else could have? My very soul had to be strong, don't get me wrong, there were many a time that I wanted to give up but my soul seemed as if it screamed, No don't give up…you are stronger, you can do it! Guess what? I am now 31 years old and still alive, yes barely, or so it seems; yet I am thankful to my inner self that I held on! What about you…does any of this, my story, hold any truths for each and every one of you in some way or another?

If you are anything like me...sometimes...I HATE being SO F***ING STRONG! Yet, I am grateful for the strength and the wisdom I have gained by my life...yes, even the sicknesses have enriched my life, although survival is a day to day task!

Maybe for you, when you think back...you were criticized, judged, or put down. You may have been the, 'bad seed', or you were 'seen but not heard'. Perhaps you were put on a pedestal, expected to live up to impossible things that no human being ever could. You may have been scared and no one comforted you...you may have been angry but were told you were not allowed to be! Maybe you were just sad but no one bothered to take notice and help you smile...even for a while. It could have been that you were looked at as a nothing, or maybe totally ignored...maybe for you it was the opposite and you were over protected with an obsessive parent. You could have just felt that you had NO control over your own life.

Any way you look at these issues...any way you slice them...they are in one form or another...ABUSE! We as a society, are so conditioned that abuse only comes in the form of bruises or sexual deviance, however most abuse is hidden inside our very essence as a human being. The truth of the matter is that abuse comes in many shapes and forms with various walls and boundaries. I hope you realize that I'm not asking you to find blame, only acceptance! For example, when I was 8 years old I became anorexic. Why? Not because I felt I was fat, nor did anyone tell me that I was, but because I felt that I had no control over my life! Refusing to eat was the ONE thing that I felt I had control over! No matter how much my family begged me to eat as death's door stood hauntingly close to me... I could control that, if nothing else!

The similar things about people like you and I are that we are fighters, and survivors! It took for me to move from my mother's to my father's to begin eating again. Why?

No...it was not because I got what I wanted. It was because I thought I would find love there...though I was sadly mistaken! In fact, I only found more abandonment, more hurt and neglect!

Although, through all of that I found one of my best friends...a true friend...one that I still have today!

So on the lighter side, everything, no matter how bad it may seem, no matter how hard it is, or helpless you feel...there is always a reason to stay strong! Yet it is through our hard, stressful lives that we became susceptible to becoming ill.

For each and every time we found ourselves in stressful situations, our bodies reacted, whether we knew it or not. We, in these situations, triggered our body's, 'fight or flight' response, which is very useful if you are face to face with a wild tiger...yet not so useful, otherwise!

However when it is used to fight stress signals that we release to our bodies, it causes irreversible damage to our immune systems, especially after prolonged periods of time. As a result, there comes a time when our body has had enough! Our immune system shuts down its' defenses...and just like magic...we become sick!

'Strength is the power within us...
Courage is the power to use it!'

Loneliness seems to be one of the ongoing feelings that we face in our day to day lives, as people with chronic illness often do. It is not the same loneliness that healthy people face but an overwhelming dread, like a dark gray cloud that follows you, no matter where you are! Over the years, I've realized that it does not go away completely, however if you understand that there are millions of people out there just like you, it may cut the loneliness to half.

Acceptance is a big part of our loneliness, as we must accept that we are not like others, healthy people, that is! For example, it was not until I STOPPED comparing myself to everyone around me that I felt some of the loneliness subside. Society in itself puts so much pressure on us to 'BE ALL WE CAN BE', yet we are being all that we can be…just to survive! It was when I accepted that I was no longer able to compare myself to others around me, for I can not be who they are nor do the things that they can do; that my loneliness started to subside. I spent so many years in denial that I couldn't figure out that to really flow with our illness we must accept it, not fight it!

In fact, it took me years to stop fighting it! I remember back just two years ago when the loneliness, the things that I could not do, the pain of trying so hard to be someone else…someone that was healthy…brought me to a suicidal state. I wanted out for I felt that NO ONE, not even me could live a life like this, and my loneliness for someone to understand…truly understand was overwhelming.

It was as if I wanted someone else to come into my body and see, feel, and be who I was on the inside…someone to know the ultimate struggles that I faced every single day. Of course, this could never be nor would I ever wish this on ANYONE, that is for sure…not even my enemies! It is now that I will share my poem with you, that I had written one, lonely night, as my tears filled the page. As you read it, I feel that you will understand why it is called: 'TRAPPED'

So here I sit once again in the middle of the night,
Wondering how to change my life to make it right
And the more I realize and understand,
I know that my sickness is in command.
For I have no control over how I feel,
Or that my life is never mine for real.
Since it has taken over my body and soul.
Stole from me, my very life as a whole.
I cannot break away from its' jagged edge,
Or the power that dangles me on its' edge.
For I have fought for many years,

Kathy M.

Thoughts of hope, anger, and many tears.
I know that within each and every day
There will be some kind of pain and dismay
I have had no choice but to live with it,
From changing my dreams to having to quit.
Since my everyday must exist around you,
Can you please tell me what I can do?.
Let me know just how to let go,
Of the anger that has grown in me so.
Give me the answer as to how I can deal,
With the horrible pain and sadness I feel
As others would offer their encouragement,
With helping hands and kindness sent.
Yet no one could know how in my life,
It's a constant battle just to survive.
As I wonder what horrible thing that I did,
To be punished for so long and just handed…
A life that holds such pain and defeat,
One that will never really be complete.
It seems that I've found all I need,
To have a happy and content life to lead.
Yet I wonder, is it really worth anything?
When my sickness holds what my fate will
bring.
I am so terribly tired of having to fight,
Each and every single day and night.

I just wish for you to leave me alone,
So that I am free to live a life on my own,
I feel that I have done my time, and more,
As you have beaten me to the very core.

You have driven me to my very end,
The eternal sickness that you send.
To God I have prayed and prayed,
But even His power you have outweighed.
So I ask with sincerity within this poem,
What is it that will make you leave my home?

Kathy M.

As I went through therapy, I realized that since I was 18 years old, I was not in acceptance but in denial...I wanted to choose life, yet I didn't know how. I had to re-evaluate my whole thinking process, and realize that the loneliness that I felt was isolation. I used to blame my dear fiancé for not spending all his time with me...for I was so lonely...couldn't he see that? Then I realized through lots of inner learning that he was not lonely, I was! WHY?

I could not expect him to be there all the time and not have a life of his own...for he is a healthy man, full of energy. It is my challenge to accept the loneliness I feel as yet another symptom of being ill. This is where support groups come in...to find a friend who can relate with you on every level, on any day. Yet that is where my beliefs in support groups ends as being a member of many at different points during my life...I find them to be very depressing and after I have walked out...I have felt nothing but hopeless and helpless.

I believe that they spend too much time on the poor us aspect instead of brainstorming to get to our inner selves and the real issues that must be discussed, after all we ALL know the symptoms, the struggles, the pain... I feel that if they focused on coping skills to get through those aspects in day to day life they may actually become a real support group! I hope that my book will be a tool for everyone to use, as they struggle through their day to day lives with illness and pain.

Don't get me wrong, there are some days that we cannot help but feeling lonely, we all know those days...the real bad ones, and on those days loneliness, sorrow and 'Why me?' are going to come. So let it out and have a good cry, let yourself go, instead of trying to be STRONG! Then when you feel a little better, that is the time to call up a friend who has this illness and let it all out. Oddly enough, you may find that they are having just as bad of a day, and together you will cheer each other up, and realize that you will be okay...you will survive, after all we are SURVIVORS!

'To choose loneliness keeps us in denial...
To choose acceptance keeps us alive!'

Right now I want to share with you something that I wrote, as I do, when I am having a bad day. I'm sure you will relate, remember this is an average page in my journal, as I have found that writing is a good outlet for me...maybe you could try it and see if it helps you. Any ways, here goes!

Dear journal,

The pain is EVERYWHERE, no one but syndromites could possibly understand. I tried to go to sleep but the pain pounds through my body, like a jackhammer eats through cement. I feel like crying, but I know it won't help. I feel like screaming but I know that won't help. Painkillers don't even help! One thing is for sure, I know every part of my body IS attached to ME. To move, roll over, stand up, sit down, and try to walk or even crawl requires agonizing effort and too much pain. Getting angry is all I can seem to do right now and so this I write. Some people, healthy people, don't know what they've got until it's gone...till they're spun into one web of pain to another. What do we do to make others realize the glory of health? We had it once, or at least I did, but now I'm to live a life of pain, disappointment and anger. Why me, I ask? Yet I know the answer...I'm supposed to learn and grow...from this I ask, how? For now I take my painkillers, gravol, and my sleeping medication, and hope by some miracle that God has mercy on me, for just a little while, until I can go to sleep! Don't smoke, I do! Don't drink coffee, I do, decaf that is, because God knows if I drink real coffee, it will send me into sweats, tremors, and heart palpitations! Anyway, my doctor says, "Don't drink a coffee or a tea after 4:00 and have your last cigarette before 6:00P.M." Well, I'll tell you, it's hard enough to live this life day after hell raising day so I'm going to do it anyway. If we change this and stop that or try all the health remedies, or 'be good'…we don't get better anyway so what the hell…might as well enjoy what little we can do with our lives since most things, "We Can't Do!" Oh sure, we look great BUT do we feel great…that is the question. It drives me crazy because we know the answer to that every minuscule moment of each and every day. Looks are not reality! If nothing else I've learned that!

Till next time, Kat

So does this hit home for any of you? You're own anger? You're own disappointment? You're own frustration? You're own pain? I wanted to share this with you because I want you to know that I am a real person, fighting to get through each and every day, just as you are. My hopes are that my book will inspire you to cope better, understand more and have the best quality of life possible.

Anger, I have found is one of the hardest feelings to cope with, as it is not the same anger that we usually feel. Usually, we are angry with someone...or something someone has said or done, where we can address this as a situation with whomever and deal with it.

The problem with our anger is that it is focused on our self...because of our illness. It is very hard to focus our anger since we can not see our illness...that is not to say we don't feel it ALL the time. This in itself can become self destructive to both our health and our self - esteem. To get angry is to stay mentally healthy but if the anger becomes overwhelming it can rule your life...which in turn only proves to make you sicker, more stressed out and frustrated.

I feel my anger comes when I feel that I've failed in something or in someone due to my illness. For example, when I see an old high school friend who is now a professional teacher, nurse etc., I feel angry, angry that I have been cheated out of my chance at living! Another example is when I feel that my children and my husband have to watch as I suffer endlessly to survive.

I'm angry also at society in their complete disregard for our illness, as they shuffle us off as though we are lazy, crazy or whatever! Disability takes the prize for me in my anger...I would have to say...since they have the nerve to deny me still my right to bring in an income, to be able to support myself and my family! Who the hell made them God? It angers me so that after all this time they think I do not qualify to all their criteria! Who would choose a life like ours? Who could fake a life like ours? Even the thought of it all is absolutely absurd, yet I'm still fighting...as I've said before I am a survivor!

The problem with having too much anger is that when it is not expressed, it then turns inward, usually at you. I'm not a good enough mother/father. I'm not a good enough wife/husband. I'm not a good enough daughter/son. I might as well not even be here for what can I do, anyway? I'm just a nuisance to everyone around me. It is due to me and my illness that my family is so worried.

Why can't I just do that, like she/he does? Why can't I ride bikes with my kids? Why can't I go swimming and have fun like everyone else in the pool? Why can't I go for a long nature hike with my family? Why can't I play baseball, volleyball, or soccer? What am I good for...nothing...might as well give it up now. Everyone whom I love would be better off without me. I don't want to live anymore if I have to live with this crap...who could even call it a life?

Does any of this sound familiar to you? I almost don't have to ask, as I know all of these

Kathy M.

feelings…which by the way are very valid. The problem is that taken in this context they are jaded…the anger has overcome you and you can't breathe. It is at this point that you must take control of the anger and as odd as this sounds get angry at your anger.

When you take back that control you no longer let yourself stay a victim of your anger but an active participant in it. I will not sit here and tell you not to get angry at your situation, your pain, your frustration but I will tell you to do a reality check on yourself, when you seem angry all the time.

Anger is a funny emotion, one that needs you to step back sometimes, just to see if what you are seeing is reality. For example, when you feel that you are good for nothing…are you really? That is not a reality of truth but a reality of the truth that you gave to your anger. Don't get me wrong…there are times when I'm so angry at my sickness, my insomnia and my life full of pills that when I try to write in my journal…all that comes is scribble! Yet, does it ever feel good to get it out…try it sometime and see if you agree…deal?

'Anger that controls you is victimizing you…

Anger that you control is strengthening you!'

18

I am not about to list ALL the symptoms that we face for there are just too many but I will say that they take their toll on us! After years of being ill, I can still be overwhelmed by how incredibly horrible I can feel and how they can come at you like a transport truck doing 8000 miles an hour.

Still to this day, I can not predict when any given symptom will hit me like a wave hitting the break wall of a pier. There is no warning...from day to day, or even hour to hour...all of a sudden it is there in full force!

Exercise, they say...yeah right...what they don't say is what you will feel like afterwards, sometimes up to days later. Doctors...just don't know what to tell us so they give orders to exercise...after all it's good for everyone...isn't it?

Don't get me wrong, I love my doctor as she is very understanding and tries her best to help me, there is only one problem...she is NOT sick! No one but us really know the scariness of your leg suddenly shaking out of control and you can not STOP it. Nobody but us knows the numbness that comes and goes or the horrible, constant ache deep within our bodies. Nobody but us knows not to leave our house without our pills, because you just never know! We are the only ones that go from test to test and specialist to specialist, in hopes that something can cure us of this ongoing craziness that has become what we know as our lives.

We hope that by some miracle that in our next blood test, our next ultrasound, our next test…they will find the answer…yet we know in our minds…we already have the answer. As disappointing as this is, we must accept ourselves as we are…but first we must learn how.

When we wake up in the morning…the afternoon…the evening, the pain is there, so we must get up to take our pills. However, once we have had a while to wake up and the pain is subsiding, we must look at our situation. It is at this time that is essential to do a thinking check. Are you angry? It was not until recently that I realized that even before I was fully awake, I was angry; angry at the pain!

What symptoms don't I have today, you may want to ask yourself. Is my stomach okay, today…how are my legs, how tired am I? After you assess your own private situation…come to the conclusion that it could be a lot worse, am I right?

Yes, there will be the days that these exercises…pardon my pun on words…it will be impossible to find that bright light. For we ALL have those days where we have no choice but to sleep, be a vegetable on the couch, and virtually become non-existent for the day…after all, we are sick!

Yet if you can make this a daily ritual, you will find that you focus less on the bad symptoms, and more on the ones that are in and out...for lack of a better word, I will call them the better symptoms...the ones that come and go!

This in turn, over some time will allow you the freedom that you need to get out of the victim role and into the living role. After all, we are all here on earth just to survive...and I'd say that we do a damn good job with what we have to work with, wouldn't you?

This will take practice but in this life we are given choices...for so long...I focused on all the bad symptoms...this got me no where but letting the illness control me! It was not until I had my crash...the lowest point in my life! I wanted out of this life yet I realized that I didn't really want to leave my loved ones...I wanted to leave me! It was at that time that I recognized myself as only being sick. I was not worthy enough...I could not possibly go on...so I felt. It was through tremendous effort and tremendous self-work that I realized the only choice...TO LIVE!

'Survival is our life...
Yet to live is our goal!'

For years I couldn't figure out how I was of any use at all to anyone including myself. I felt like I was in a huge black hole filled with dirt. To be honest I used to wish someone would just cover the hole and bury me. The thoughts of trying to climb out was overwhelming, as it felt as if everytime I would climb even a little, digging my hands into the dirt as I went, more dirt would fall...as my grasp would slip and I'd fall back to where I started. It seemed hopeless that I could ever get to the top...even still I couldn't give up...though so many parts of me at so many different times screamed at me to.

No...I would not give up! This is how depression feels. Yet even though I am taking medication for depression...for so long that was how my life felt. I couldn't grasp the fact that I could be worth anything to myself...let alone anyone else. I remember going to a therapy workshop run through the hospital, called, "Learning how to set goals." She could not help me, as my 'goal' was to accept my illnesses...she couldn't even tell me where to start. I admit that it was not the traditional goal setting, yet in my life...if I was to have one...I had to find a way.

It was through my wonderful counselor that I recognized that I was looking at the wrong things. Yes, we all have to set goals in life...but we must set realistic goals...not impossible ones. I am forever grateful to her as she taught me that I am worth loving, but most of all I am worth loving MYSELF.

You see, what I refused to see was my accomplishments...not what kind of car I had, not what my house looked like, not whether I was married or single, not if I had a job...but the important things in my life.

Everyday I accomplish something, no matter how small or big...I could always find something that I had accomplished within each and every day. She helped me realize that even my day of sleeping was an accomplishment for I was resting, taking care of myself, and that meant that I was helping myself. Once I started to change my way of thinking, I realized that I have accomplished a lot of wonderful things in my life.

If you think about your life this way...you will also find that you have made amazing accomplishments in your life. Just trying to get from day to day for us...is a huge accomplishment.

Reward yourself, for living our life is, in itself an on going accomplishment. Did you make it out of bed? Did you brush your hair? Did you get dressed? Did you have a shower? Just making it out of bed is an accomplishment for the ill. Realize that we are not like others and to do these simple tasks on a day to day basis is next to impossible, yet we persevere and with all our effort...we do them!

Of course, some days are worse than others...but take a look at what you do on any given day...now smile for you are special in all that you do...we all are! It was through months of counseling that I realized that my goals, even as small as they maybe to someone, who is healthy, are an important part of my well being.

I learned how to set goals for myself, as a 'sick' person rather than goals that healthy people would set. Sure it is important to look into the future and set a goal for where we would like to be in 5 years from now...yet it is also important that this be realistic. To say that in 5 years from now your goal is to be cured is to set yourself up for disappointment, as there is no realism to it. To say that in 5 years from now you want to the best you can be...is a goal. The best you can be mentally will bring you to the best you can be physically, for sure.

I learned to set about five goals per day, the most important...to get out of bed. Yes, that is a goal, as simplistic as it may be...it is a goal of mine everyday! I have learned to make lists the day before of things I must do...keep it simple, 2 things at most...the rest are minor goals per day and if I don't reach them...oh well...I look at what I DID DO that day!

I've learned that if I don't do this or that...it DOES NOT reflect on me as a person...I am still a good person, just a sick one, that's all. Think back and remember ALL of the times you have put yourself down, when it really had NOTHING to do with YOU at all, for whatever it was or wasn't, it had to do with the sickness...not you...the person! How may of you can identify?

'Accomplishments are fulfilling...
Realizing them is life rewarding!'

As human beings we can be so ridiculous…almost crazy…we don't like to ask for help, at least I didn't…which led me to my crash, and almost suicide. For the love of you…ask for help!

I remember when I would actually refuse help, as I was not going to give in, I could handle everything all by myself because I felt that if accepted help and people really knew how desperately I NEEDED HELP, they would think lesser of me as a person. WRONG!

Since I have learned to accept and even ask for help, I've improved my quality of life phenomenally. I felt that because I was sick that I could not show my weakness as people would think I was just 'USING' my illness as an excuse not to do something. Sick, or not, let us face reality, not one person can handle everything on their own…and for those of us that are sick…we need ALL the help we can get.

In order to let go of the guilt or shame that I felt by 'ASKING' for help, I had to make a conscious effort to accept myself for who I was…not what I could or could not do. I had to start recognizing that I am a good person, regardless of my medical condition…and if my house was a shambles…well, so be it! If I slept all day…well, so be it! If I did absolutely nothing all day, which I might say is the hardest thing that anyone person can do…(yet we are forced to)...then so be it. It did not change the person that I am, nor will it ever! Can you relate to these feelings?

Stop the guilt! Stop the shoulds in your life because you can find that you're shoulding all over yourself. When you give in, you are not giving in to weakness; you are giving in to yourself. Something that the whole world could do a lot more of...don't you think?

'To ask for and seek help is to love one's soul...

Yet not to, is self-deprivation to one's soul!'

With all that is wrong with us physically, it astonishes me that the medical practitioners, the researchers have not caught the play yet. It is as if THEY are in denial! How many things can go wrong with us before they begin to take us seriously, as real people with real illnesses?

Still, after being ill for so many years, I have come across many of doctors...for that fact many of people that don't believe that I am sick! Do I have to be on my deathbed, pumping morphine into me every four hours to make them realize...I'm telling the truth...for crying out loud!

For one thing, there are so many illnesses that we come down with along our journey of sickness...that there are too many different names thrown around...who would believe it? For example...first you may be diagnosed with Chronic Fatigue Immune Deficiency Syndrome, as I was. Then some months later, different symptoms appear that does not match their medical criteria...and you are diagnosed with Fibromyalgia, as I was. Then some months later you are diagnosed with Myo-Fascial Pain Syndrome. Then you are diagnosed with Irritable Bladder Syndrome...and on and on it goes!

When will they ever take us seriously...please, I'm begging...TAKE US SERIOUSLY! We seem to have more knowledge then the doctors, themselves...for we are the sufferers.

Frankly, it sickens me even more that they have not put the correlation of all of our 'SYNDROMES' together. It is a disease...when, how long do we have to wait before they figure this out? Why can't they put this all together, Lord knows we have...scratch out all the symptomoligy and labeling and call it a disease. As I know very well, it is a degenerative illness, which classifies it as a disease. For that matter, when are they going to wake up and tell us that these ARE degenerative sicknesses' not to be sloughed off as syndromes or symptomoligy. We are the sufferers, damn them, any ways!

How tired are you of learning that you have, yet, another medical problem of some kind? I know I am! Not a doctor alive can convince me that my problems are not degenerative, for in just the last year, I feel that my quality of life has been reduced by fifty percent. So...how long will it take these highly qualified, well trained, informative people of the medical profession to come out with this news? Are they afraid to tell us that we have a disease...no, in my opinion they have not figured this out yet?

They are not the ones suffering, are they? Along with our everyday extravaganza that we must endure, we must put up with their lack of ability to add it all up. Guess what? I had figured this out long ago. Not because I am a genius, nor do I profess to be...but because I am a sufferer, who like yourself, I am sure, knows that month after month, we progressively get worse! Our quality of life gets less and less as our limitations become more and more.

Rehabilitation...my ass! What, just because we cannot 'DIE' from our suffering, makes it not worth their while to research it as a progressive disease? NOT! It needs to be recognized and researched as a disease, for it contains lists and lists of problems and symptoms which make it valid to be a disease...a recognizable one. Wouldn't it be nice to say one or two words (something that the average person will understand) to explain our suffering! Call it whatever they want, but stop denying us... and society of the reality of what we must endure, every single day of our lives.

Even, to call it "The Internal Eternal Disease," would be better than syndrome this...syndrome that...for a syndrome is just stashed away, treated the best way they know how, and locked away as hush, hush. Heaven forbid they look deeper into the combination of problems! I have not had one clinical specialist tell me that as year after year goes by, my quality of life will be reduced, nor have they ever given me any hope that I will recover...so what is it? Just cope...deal with it...rest...listen to your body...don't overdue things...don't do too much...take these pills. No cure, yet it never is referred to as a disease!

It has been a real chore not to scream and yell, demand answers and more information on my syndromes! Yet, that is why I feel the importance to write this in my book...maybe, just maybe I will get SOMEONE'S attention. After all, we are not crazy, lazy...we did not choose this, nor would we wish this on anyone.

It is my hopes that this will get their attention...after all we can diagnose ourselves. To a greater or lesser degree...for we are the ones who know what we go through...each and every day. For, as far as I can tell...the longer you have one thing diagnosed, the sooner you are to getting another illness\syndrome...that is irreversible.

SOMEONE must get their attention...don't you agree? It is not my intent to make anyone mad. Yet they MUST begin to open their eyes to reality...OUR reality!

This is not to say that it will change our day to day suffering...because, of course, we all know that it will not, yet it may make us feel more validated as people and the pain that we endure. This in turn will make society more aware...and as if a miracle happened, with only a few words...our suffering will not go unnoticed…and viola we have REAL validation.

First for ourselves! Then for society…then for all whom have doubted our suffering throughout our illness.

'To suffer through this life is one thing…
But to suffer unnoticed is quite another!'

I would like to return to the lighter side once again, one which will show you the incredible irony that we face each and every day. The side which can make us laugh, just a little at our illness and ourselves. You may not have looked at things in your life at this angle before, yet I am confident that you will be able to relate and even laugh at the irony of it all.

What is Chronic Fatigue Immune Deficiency Syndrome? It is a condition that consists of incredible pain and FATIGUE, that only we the sufferers, can possibly relate to...yet how many people have you come across who tell you that they MUST have it, too! They go on to tell you that they are constantly tired and feel like they are just not themselves these days. This is a prime example of the irony, since not one healthy person could EVER know how very tired we really are. I had gotten so sick of hearing this that I almost punched a woman...only to find out that she in fact was suffering and wanted to know more about it, from me. A classic case of the irony...and a perfect chance to laugh at myself!

If you are so VERY tired all day long, yet you CAN NOT sleep at night, you are experiencing the irony of our illness, since when you think logically...how can we be so tired ALL the time, yet have such sleeping problems? Wait, there is more...as if we were

33

nocturnal creatures, we can ALL in fact, sleep wonderfully during the day...irony it must be!

I'm always amazed that I look so well on the outside, or so I have been told, repeatedly. Come on say it with me, as I know you have heard it as well, "You're looking good today!" Yet even as we smile and politely say, "Thank you," our insides are in agony. God help us if it is one of those days that we feel as if we have just been run over by a transport truck, not just once...but twice, doing 200 miles an hour. Irony at it's finest...don't you think? Yet as if we do not feel bad enough...we have others telling us that if we can live STRESS FREE lives, we will be fine. Oh, that is simple, and absolutely achievable in the society we are living in, don't you think? Somebody stop the irony, already!

I can safely say that each and every one of you reading this book has gone through numerous, annoying tests to find out what is wrong with you. You know the blood tests, the pee tests, the poke tests, the x-rays, the dye tests, ultrasounds...blah, blah, blah! Ironically so, all the tests prove you to be healthy...not a thing wrong with you, am I right? Here is where I find the irony...although we can barely survive day by monotonous day we could in fact, according to the medical tests run a marathon! Are you finding the irony yet?

Then as we search on for answers, only to find none…we decide that we must be crazy, right? So off to the psychiatrist we go, spilling our guts, once again. Guess what? The psychiatrist concludes that our mental health is just fine! So we must just be lazy, as there is absolutely no other sane explanation! Here is where the irony lies, as not one of us would ever choose to feel this way, yet we were chosen!

Now… we are lost, sick, and tired, but now we are depressed, as well. Anti-depressants are the answer to our survival now, yet due to our illnesses, we must be very careful what we take. Since as a syndromite any medication may have reverse effects or even unheard of side effects…we must take all precautions and pray! In fact, what should actually help us, may backfire and harm us…ironically contradictory, or what?

As we have all been told, we must exercise, in moderation, of course! What is that, I ask with complete bewilderment, as during the entire 14 years as a syndromite, I have not found that fine line between moderation and torture! You see it is only us who can possibly understand that there is no moderation, no in between…only functional or non-functional. I do agree that we need some type of exercise, yet it can not be on a scheduled routine for we do not work that way. Even when we do exercise, we can not tell how much is too much, as we ask ourselves that scary question, "When will I crash?" Yes, we know it is coming, in its own timely fashion, don't we...when will become the primary question? Once again in our day to day lives, irony shows its face.

Has any one of you gone to the doctor and he/she asks you what your symptoms are? Your answer goes something like this, "Well, right now my arm is throbbing, yesterday, my leg was numb, the day before that, my neck was so sore that I could not lift it from the pillow. My hands are swollen to twice their original size and my stomach is bloated and in pain, and when I woke up this morning, my chest hurt so bad that I could have sworn that I had elephants standing on me!" You are a syndromite in the grips of irony!

When a registered nurse does not believe that you are actually sick, until she sees it on television, you are without a doubt living the irony that we go through every day, don't you agree?

I can remember the very first day that I was told that I had an illness called Chronic Fatigue Immune Deficiency Syndrome. The doctor went on to tell me that there was nothing that they could do for me, but not to worry, for it was not contagious. As I left the office with a sigh of relief, knowing that I could not give it to anyone else, I suddenly felt as if a huge brick had fallen on my head…then how the hell did I get it? Even after extensive research, I still do not understand this concept. If you can relate to my bewilderment, then you too, are suffering from syndromite irony!

I'd like to share with you, the event in my life that made me see the irony of my illness. It was after I could cry no more (or so I thought) that it became clear, that my tears changed to laughter. Maybe after hearing my story, you will choose to look closer at your own story, find the irony and have a few laughs.

Like most of you as syndromites, I can not work due to the lists and lists of symptoms that come upon me whenever they choose. Like many of you, I have applied for disability. I have been denied 3 times due to the question of the severity of my illness. That on its' own is ironic, yet it gets much better. Due to the fact that I can not work, my finances are poor, and as a mother and a renter of someone else's property, financially I was sinking like the Titanic. My lifeboats did arrive however, named mom and grandma. So generous were my lifeboats that they helped me to buy a home of my own, of course without an income of my own, I couldn't qualify for the mortgage. So my mother and I became co-owners of my home while my fiancé paid the mortgage.

Kathy M.

It was now necessary to get life insurance, and with me in my late twenties, and my mother in her fifties in good health, we figured there would be no problems. Wrong! My mother qualified with flying colors, yet after searching through at least 20 insurance companies, I was denied!

It was about that time that I felt that I might just lose my mind, whatever mind I had left at this point. As my frustration felt very familiar to me, I soon realized that this irony was only the beginning of a life long lesson for me.

It was then that I realized that I must share my experiences, good, bad, or indifferent, with others like myself. I knew that I needed to find the positive side and help others to do the same, as life as we know can become way too cruel…if we let it.

Even more ironic…I used my denial letters from the insurance companies to fight for my disability…only to receive my third denial letter from disability. Now that is ironic, there is no denying that…no pun intended!

"To laugh through our suffering…
Gives us hope that we can still go on!"

Have you ever been having a real bad day...you know the ones that I mean, where you feel like you are on death's doorstep...and you get hit with this overwhelming fear? If I'm like this now, how bad will I feel in a year from now? The scariest part of those days for me is that I really don't know the answer...no one does. Yet as amazing as it is we survive, for myself with a lot of crying, and we live to endure yet another day.

Do you realize the courage we have, our inner strength is astounding...we are astounding people! I can not tell you what you will feel like tomorrow let alone in a year, nor do I know for myself. However, what I can tell you is that you and me have to live and think day by day. That is our survival guide, for tomorrow one never knows...not even healthy people do.

We must learn how to live for the moments and cherish them. The good times, the laughs, the things that make us smile...the things that touch our heart. For even though we are ill...we are not dead, though sometimes we wonder! Find the simple things in life and take them in with great passion...as this is what life is all about. Have you ever noticed that a simple smile or a laugh can make your day? It is on the bad days that we must learn to hold on, keep it simple, and most important love ourselves!

Why, you may be asking…because we are special people…what healthy person do you know that has the inner strength, the compassion for others, the ability to endure endless pain that has both the emotional and physical tolerance that we do? Any way you look at these questions…we come out on top, even though it certainly does not feel that way.

Who else gets to sit out of that stressful rat race called life? Who else gets to notice the very first bud on a flower or a tree? Who else gets to see the first leaf change color in the fall? WE DO!

These are the kind of things we must focus on, for without a focus…what are we doing here? We also get to do a lot of self-learning and self-teaching, self-sacrificing and self-evaluation. Let's face facts…we have a lot of time to fill, yet if we can grow within ourselves…we are here on this earth, doing what we are supposed to be doing.

Every day we learn tolerance, patience, humbleness and more about our faith…faith that we can get through another day.

It has been my faith in knowing my God and knowing my strength…that has kept me going…day after day, and year after year. When I refer to God as mine…of course He is also yours, yet did you know that He lives inside each and every one of us? Our faith, our learning is actually His, too…for He is living through us…each experience becomes His experience, too…for He is not in human form…as Jesus was!

When we pray, we are praying for His strength, His wisdom, and His help…through our own mind, body and spirit. When we think we can no longer endure…it is us…us who keeps us going, us that does the learning and us that finds the answers. Please don't get me wrong God is with us everywhere we are and He helps us…but not without our own self work…our inner strength. We are his children…and if you are lucky enough to have children…you know that we can teach them as best as we can…but ultimately the answers to their problems, their decision to grow and learn, can ONLY come from them.

I find this interesting as we are His children…and he must learn to let us go…make our mistakes…and grow. Is that not what we do with our children? We supply them with the tools for making the right and wrong decisions in their life, yet we must let them go, and it is through letting go that we…as parents learn, too. I do not believe in religion or church…for that is not how you reach God…for He can be talked to at anytime…and believe it or not when we ask Him for answers or guidance, or strength…it is within ourselves that we feel that power! Yes, I believe our strength and our answers are found…yet only when we try to help ourselves. It is up to us whether we put these answers into action…that we find relief…why…because He is living through our experiences, our love, our mistakes, quite simply our lives.

I do not believe in sin as I feel it is a word widely misused. It is simply a mistake…to help us grow…as we venture along our spiritual path. It is our gut, our instinct that tells us we are headed in the wrong direction, and it is this I believe…that is God in ourselves, telling us that whatever road we may be choosing is the wrong one for us…you may call it intuition.

My hopes are not to make people dislike my opinions or me. Yet, no matter what religion, no matter what church you go to, I feel the need to tell people that it is not by feeling like a bad person, or a sinner, that is going to make you feel better. What do you think?

Yet to think…to really think…if you have made a mistake in your life, which we all have made many…to feel bad about yourself (like you have committed a sin)…is not what is going to help you.

Loving   yourself…accepting yourself…looking deep within yourself…even getting mad at God, is what will make us continue to grow as people. To believe that we are sinners, just because we have made mistakes, in my perception…is totally wrong…and we have missed the whole purpose of being down here on earth.

Yet to blame God for our misfortunes, our bad health, and remain victims of life is also totally wrong. In doing this…we do not take responsibility for our own actions, as we constantly look for someone or something to blame the bad stuff on. To grow as a person, as a soul, as an entity all our own we must learn to look deeper into our spirituality…that is to say and ask …who are we really?

Who we are really…in my opinion…are special, intelligent, creative beings…here to live our lives the best way we know how. What is the best way we know how…to have faith in ourselves…therefore creating our own individual spiritual journey. Let us face the facts…without faith in ourselves and without growing spiritually…we would stay victims of our illness…forever!

Let me share with you now, my Father…my God…so you may get a deeper understanding of what I mean:

Father's Love Letter

My Child

You may not know me, but I know everything about you…

I know when you sit down and when you rise up…

I am familiar with all your ways…

Even the very hairs on your head are numbered…

For you were made in my image…

In me you live and move and have your being…

For you are my offspring…

I knew you even before you were conceived…

I chose you when I planned creation…

You were not a mistake…

For all your days are written in my book…

I determined the exact time of your birth and where you would live…

You are fearfully and wonderfully made…

I knit you together in your mother's womb…

And brought you forth on the day you were born…

I have been misrepresented by those who do not know me…

I am not distant and angry, but am the complete expression of love…

And it is my desire to lavish my love on you…

Simply because you are my child and I am your father…

I offer you more than your earthly father ever could…

For I am the perfect father…

Every good gift you receive comes from my hand…

For I am your provider and I meet all your needs...

My plan for your future has always been filled with hope...

Because I love you with an everlasting love...

My thoughts towards you are as endless as the sand on the seashore...

And I rejoice over you with singing...

I will never stop doing good to you...

For you are my treasured possession...

I desire to establish you with all my heart and my soul...

And I want to show you great and marvelous things...

If you seek me with all your heart, you shall find me...

Delight in me and I will give you all the desires of your heart...

For it is I who gave you those desires...

I am able to do more for you than you could possibly imagine...

For I am your greatest encourager...

I am also the Father who comforts you in all your troubles...

When you are brokenhearted, I am close to you...

As a shepherd carries a lamb, I have carried you close to my heart...

One day I will wipe away every tear from your eye...

And will take away all the pain you have suffered here on this earth...

I am your Father, and I love you even as I love my son, Jesus...

For in Jesus, my love for you is revealed...

He is the exact representation of my being...

He came to demonstrate that I am for you, not against you...

And to tell you that I am not counting your sins...

Jesus died so that you and I could be reconciled...

His death was the ultimate expression of my love for you...

I gave up everything I loved so that I might gain your love...

If you receive the gift of my son Jesus, you receive me...

And nothing will ever separate us again...

Come home and I'll throw the biggest party heaven has ever seen...

I have always been Father, and will always be Father...

My question is...Will you be my child?...

I am waiting for you...

Love Dad

This is my bible, one that truly makes sense to me...what about you? In my interpretation of His letter I see Him as part of me, my inner soul...my inner being. Without my faith that

He lives inside me...I feel I could not have made it this far, yet this is not to say that if my belief does not coincide with yours, your faith is wasted.

When I first read this letter I cried for I could feel His power inside me...I could feel His love wash over me, through me, and around me, like a tidal wave as it hits the land. I realized that in every inch of my life...He was there...helping me with all His might...yet it was I that stood through my trials and tribulations, on this earth throughout my life.

He led me from within, as He is part of my very soul, the essence of my very being, and without this inner strength I could not bear a life such as ours...could you?

Our life is what we make it, yet isn't it nice to feel the power of true love...living in every inch of us...keeping us strong...enduring our pain. I talk to Him all the time as even through my words I feel clarity and reassurance, love and gentleness. God is not to be feared, for to fear God is to fear ourselves, and to fear ourselves we cannot grow, spiritually or emotionally! Don't you agree?

'To stifle our spirituality is to fear our God...
Yet to grow in spirit is to love Him...
While also trusting and loving ourselves!'

Kathy M.

Sometimes, while I watch others ride their bikes, play sports and just have 'NORMAL' energy, an overwhelming sadness washes over me…for I know in my life there are limitations. Some days there seems so many…you can't help those tears that come to your eyes and silently fall down your cheeks. It is on those particular days, that we wonder who it is that we have become, but most importantly…right then, who could we have become? I can only answer to you that what I know…we must let our old self go! The healthy person that you once knew is gone…yet only in the physical sense, but you must say goodbye.

When I first realized this, I did nothing but cry, weep and sob. Moans filled my cries and tears filled my eyes, for what was I now…who was I now? Even as I write this I feel a sense of sadness rush through me like a gust of wind that rattles a bird nest out of its tree.

At this time, I am going to share with you, the poem that my dear friend wrote, as she too, is chronically ill. This was written on one of her 'BAD' days. It is entitled, I AM THE GHOST:

No one listens
And no one really cares
Left on the side of the road
Litter
Garbage
An animal hit and left to die

Alone and tired of begging
For that scrap
A penny for your suffering
A nickel if you pretend you're not
I am the Ghost
That walks among you
The gutter you don't want to see
Is where I live
I am the grateful
For nothing and for everything
The dullness behind my eyes
Because you have stolen all that I am
And won't dignify what's been left
The world has turned its' back
Has shown me I am dispensable
Raise up my voice naught
It has fallen deaf
Because now
I am invisible
Author: Nancy Ferren

Life for us is different now...as our future holds a darker reality, one of pain and anguish. So we must say farewell to the lives we once knew and hold them tight in our memories...for that is what that life is now...memories! Yet we all have very great ones that live close to our heart, in fact it is some of those memories that we will find our strength to move on. We will move on as we make our new life, one with deeper meaning, harder choices and simpler thinking.

It is our thoughts that keep us who we are...not our physical health! I have not changed my personality, my values, or my life dreams. You need to recognize this as true for you, also...otherwise you will not be able to accept your illness...it will take control.

I would like you to think back to the way you were before you became ill...did the same things interest you? Did the same things make you laugh, cry and indifferent? If you are like me...your answers will have been yes...am I right?

Nothing can change who you are on the inside...not even an illness, or in our case illnesses! Whenever I feel that sadness, I say, "STOP!" That is what we must learn to do, for that kind of thinking leads to victim thinking...which leads us down a sad road. I know you don't want to be there, for I know that we are all deserving of the happy road.

This kind of thinking is just not limited to the ill but the healthy, too. For example, I use it to help my kids, when they need to realize what they have...not what they do not! After all they have their health! It is hard to say that final farewell, that last goodbye to 'THE OLD YOU', yet it is absolutely necessary to your well being. I only know this because I fought it for years and years, in what I like to call my limbo stage. I went from trying so very hard to being like everyone else and dying in bed with unbelievable pain. For years I actually pulled this life off…yet what kind of life was it?

It was a life of bitterness towards those who couldn't understand me. It was a life filled with misery. It was a life filled with contempt at others. It was a life that I lived feeling like a person being torn to shreds. It was a life of fooling others…or was it?

Who did I really fool? At the end of the day no one else paid physically or mentally for what I had done. At the end of the day no one saw my tears. At the end of the day no one felt my heart ache just to be 'ME', again. It was me…just me, who I was trying to fool…guess what? It can not be done. Through all those years, it was I who paid for wanting, trying, yearning to be that old me! Why, I wonder now…why didn't I just let go? It was then that I thought if I let go I would lose myself. It was then that I felt that if I was sick…or let myself be I would be alone! I was alone then…not now!

I'm sure anyone reading this can relate to me, so if you haven't said goodbye…just do it! The relief you will feel is amazing, the power you will feel is astounding, and the joy you will feel…could almost make you dance! Well, I said, "Almost!" When you make the solid decision to move on…you will, with amazing clarity and tremendous strength.

If you have already moved on…can you relate? Do you realize the love and acceptance you have given to yourself? Even through the bad days, you have made the choice to take the happy road…one with a future, unique to yourself…courageous and brave!

'To say goodbye to the old you…
Is to welcome truth with open arms!'

As we do welcome ourselves the way we are…we soar into a world of reality…our new reality, or what I like to call the rules of our life! These rules are not all bad, in fact some are almost nice. Who else do you know that is SUPPOSED to do nothing?

In our new way of life we must find…and live by…our limitations. This is not to say that we do nothing, yet we do only what we can do and be proud of it. We can only figure out our own limitations, by trial and error. For example, one day when my kids were younger, I tried doing a cartwheel to show them how to do it…well, you can imagine the pain! That night when I got into bed, more like fell, I couldn't figure out why my entire left side was pounding…almost screeching in pain. As I went over the day's events in my head…I began to laugh, as I remembered what I had done. So for future reference…I am limited from doing cartwheels, or any kind of gymnastics, again!

If we go past our limitations we pay the cost, no matter what it is that we did, however, you must also remember to live a little…once in a while! I guess what I mean by this is to weigh out the event as opposed to the cost…sometimes, some things are worth it. After all, we are not dead…yet…and to live under too strict of limits can drive you crazy, even nuts. I remember saying to my girlfriends, "If I have to lay on this couch for one more night...I'm goona lose it!" So, as a result, I went out that night had some drinks and let loose! I know what your question is...did I pay for it? You bet I did, but to me at that point, it was worth it...for sometimes you just have to say, "What the f***?" Do it any ways, and pay the consequences...the important part is that it be up to YOU what you will pay for and what YOU will not.

This is where my guilt used to creep in on me...for I would feel that I had to go to this family dinner or that friend's house. Finally, I realized that the family would not fall apart without me, nor did my friend's house fall down because I did not go!

It is during this time...as you set your limitations...that you may lose touch with friends...and even family. Yet, what you must always remember is that if they can not accept you for who you really are...then they are not worth it. Believe me, it will not take forever to find people who love you just the way you are...after all, isn't everyone just the way they are.

I remember when I was first ill, my cousins whom I'd grown up with...much like a sister and brother to me...didn't even acknowledge my sickness. Just recently, my cousin came up to me, wanting an ear to listen, because she is now clinically depressed...did I listen? I might have until she told me that before she became this way, she thought people 'like that' were just making it up. Gee, that comment made me feel so special...thanks for sharing...NOT!

My mother-in-law to be, thought that I was taking advantage of her son, since many of times he would have the three children with him, while I was at home in bed.

My own father, whom I cut relations with...if you knew him you would know why, would ask me if I was still sick...what do you think?

Accepting our limitations may mean some real life changes...yet without these, are you really being true to yourself. Living by these limitations is absolutely frustrating, yet at the same time peaceful. How?

Once you decide to live by your set of rules...you can be more to yourself and those you love both emotionally and spiritually. You will see more clearly what is important in your life, and you will have more to give to those things. Don't get me wrong...it is still difficult to be sick all the time, yet it seems more normal...when you actually accept it!

In a lot of ways it is easier to find YOU once you have taken these steps because the things you value most in life will become crystal clear. You will have stronger feelings about certain things and weaker ones for things not so important in life! In a way...we are the lucky ones because we can become one with our soul without having the confusion of all the 'STUFF' that healthy people have to mix them up.

All we have to do is survive…just plain…survive! That in itself, sometimes seems impossible, yet every night when we go to bed…we wake up the next day…to have survived, yet another day! To know that we just have to survive…is sometimes a great relief…at least it is to me…what about you?

'To live our lives in reality is sometimes hard…

Yet to live a life of half-truths becomes impossible!'

Just to survive brings me back to the lighter side, once again…since syndromites and jobs mix like oil and water! NOT! What do you think?

When I was first ill, I was only eighteen years of age, working many jobs only to get fired soon after, as I was too slow. You see back then, there was even less knowledge about our illness as there is now…and after a few months of sleeping and resting, I could take no more of doing nothing…I am sure you can relate.

So after being fired from many jobs, I landed a job at a local grocery store. My bigger plan was to work for awhile, then probably go into college or university to become a qualified Early Childhood Educator. As I worked in the grocery store, once again, my plans changed rather abruptly, as I was transferred from department to department because I was too slow!

Well, if you knew me back then I had quite the attitude and frankly I was sick of hearing this. After all, I WAS going as fast as I could go. Finally, I ended up in the bakery department and my apologies go out to a very kind man who received a horrendous loaf of bread! You see, we baked the bread and if a customer wanted it sliced we had the slicing machine to do it. This should have made it an easy task…not on this day. This particular gentleman requested to have his bread sliced…sure not a problem…or so I thought at that moment.

In actual fact…it was not the slicer that gave me the problem. It was the bag that was only minuscule larger than the loaf itself. That poor man watched, speechless, as I fought to get that bread inside that bag and when I finally won the battle of the bread bag…I passed him a loaf of bread that looked like it had been hit by a tornado! With a few pieces missing, others turned sideways, and some completely upside down. I distinctly remember his look of bewilderment as he shook his head and left with a loaf of bread that looked as if…and actually was in a war zone!

Even as I write this, I can picture it so clear in my head that the whole scenario sends me bursting into laughter. Anyway sir, if in fact you ever read this book…I am truly sorry and I thank you for your kindness on that day.

You see I was in fact suffering from syndromitis but did not realize it yet! The only facts that I knew then, was even the simplest of instructions sounded like a foreign language to me. Combine that with no co-ordination and complete exhaustion, I felt I was being run off my feet. The term run off my feet became literal, only weeks later as I collapsed from lifting a tray of bread. That was it…like oil and water…no career for me!

That is what confuses most people…it is not that we do not want to work…it is that we can not work! We, as syndromites, must conjure up enough energy to get out of bed every day, which is in fact more energy than I ever remember using for absolutely anything before we were sick, don't you agree? Hell, I couldn't even be a stripper to make money, even if I wanted to…dancing…spinning around a pole? Halfway through my first song they would have to scrape me off the stage…boy…what money I could make!

I could work as a secretary, forgetting messages, spilling coffee, scheduling important meetings with people's names I could not remember! The only thing I could always remember to schedule would be naptime, and the last time that I checked, they don't allow scheduling for that!

Just imagine what our resumes as a syndromite would look like…

Dear Sir,

I know I would be an asset for your company since I can @$%&$, sleep, @^#**, lay down, %&$**. I can sometimes read my own handwriting and am very good at #$&*%**, and sleeping. Oh yes, I forgot to mention that I am an experienced syndromite and therefore can not be depended on daily, hourly, or any time in between! I realize that you have many applications to go through but

Kathy M.

none can sleep...or not sleep the way that I
can! It pains me, no...it really does...to think
of any one else taking more medication; I mean
of any one else getting this position, lying
down. I feel that it is my obligation to let you
know that I can not sit, stand, or function for
any length of time, as I may very well collapse
on my...asset for the job!

Thank you and good night.

Now that is a resume, original for sure...do
you think we would get the job? It is crucial to
me, as I write this book, that every one of you
who are sick, understand that is not you that
chose to be this way. You must realize that for
whatever the reason, we as syndromites are the
chosen. It is absolutely essential that you do not
equate your self worth with a job title...for you
are an important individual...just the way you
are! To be able to walk on the lighter side with
me, you must realize that in your very soul, you
are an amazing and unique individual. You and
I are the chosen...we are special and wonderful
for all kinds of reasons, and as you read this
book I hope you will agree!

'To feel the need to have a title in life...
Is to disregard yourself worth as an
individual.'

People with lives like ours; evolving of pain and enduring hardships...must learn a healthy type of self-talk. To learn this could be the difference between life and death. We already know the things that we can not be...but what about the things we can be. For example, it would be unrealistic for any one of us to go to bed at night and tell ourselves that we will not be sick tomorrow. Yet, for us to go to bed and tell ourselves that we will have a good day tomorrow is in the realm of possibilities.

A good day, does not mean that we will be pain free, nor does it mean that we will do anything, except keeping our spirit healthy!

What we say to ourselves is what makes us who we are...not what we know of ourselves. I know I am sick and disabled in a lot of ways, yet if I tell myself that I'm well in my heart...then, I will be. Just because I am sick does not change who I am on the inside...but it can if I let it. I spent years bitter and sad because I was sick. I told myself that I was good for nothing all the time, but was I really good for nothing?

No, of course not...so with a lot of self-talk, a lot of support, and a little more wisdom, I began to like myself. I began to see my life differently, and with that I began to see that I am a good person...even though I am sick! What an amazing discovery this was for me...can any one of you relate? Once I started seeing myself in a whole new way and continued with positive thinking, I actually began to love myself.

I'd see how clearly that the old suicidal me was not really wanting out of my life…just out of my body. I figured out that our bodies are just that…places for our souls at this time, here on earth. If you look at our lives in this way, we can handle the sickness of our bodies because it in no way diminishes or defines our very being, our spirit, or our soul.

There have been so many times that I've said to my husband-to-be, "If you want to leave me, I will understand, for I know that you won't be leaving me, just my sickness." Sometimes, I have gone as far as telling him to run like hell, 'cause I know if I had the chance to run…I'd be gone! Yet, when I am saying these things it is not my intent to slam myself or put myself down in any way…it is just the separation that I have found for me and my sickness.

No longer does my physical body own how I feel, emotionally. No longer when I wake up in unbelievable pain is my day ruined! In some ways you could actually say that I have divorced my emotional ties with my body! We fought too much; my body would take over…so I left!

To try and teach yourself to talk to yourself in a healthy way, is not easy yet very rewarding. Not only will you find yourself a happier person, but a much calmer one, as well. Here is how I began my personal journey of emotional well being.

First of all...I must be on anti-depressants, or I WILL be suicidal. For me, there is no way around it, as life is not worth living without them. This is not to say that everyone who is suffering MUST be on them, because that is not necessarily the fact.

I figured out through therapy that I have been depressed my whole life...well at least since I was 5 years old. That is the first time that my memory comes to me that I became depressed, as I was standing on my grand parent's lawn...waiting for my daddy to come pick me up for the day. I waited and waited, standing on the corner, looking down the street, watching car after car drive by. Each one that would come down the road, I would think to myself, this one will be him...and it was after hours had gone by, my mom called him to find that he was still home and had no intention of seeing me that day.

After she told me...he wasn't coming, I sat on the beautiful green grass that my grandpa took such pride in, and wept for hours. It is through therapy that I was able to get off that corner, for throughout my whole life that little girl was still waiting for her perfect daddy to come and love her. So as near as I can figure, that is when my life of chemical imbalance started.

I remember when I went to live at my dad's, when I wanted to kill myself by not eating at my mom's...I still wanted to kill myself. I used to sit by the train tracks and wonder if anyone would even care if I died...at one point when I lived there, I tried to suffocate myself with a pillow. Guess what? It doesn't work! I used to sob by myself and say, "All I want to do is die!"

So if any of this rings a bell to you or you find yourself dreaming of ways to kill yourself...get to a doctor IMMEDIATELY! That is clinical depression...and unbeknownst to ignorant people out there...you can't just snap out of it. Please do not feel bad about yourself if you need anti-depressants, for that does not make you less of a person, only more for realizing that you need help! I find that is rare for people who are chronically ill, not to be overwhelmed by depression as no matter how strong our spirit is, let's face the facts...we live a life of pain and suffering...who wouldn't be depressed by that?

So...once you figure out whether you are in need of some help with pills...then you must figure out how you are thinking. This may sound silly, yet it is a very real problem for everyone, especially people who suffer on a daily basis. The way that I figured out that I was a negative thinker was to have a note pad with me at all times, and any negative thought that I had, I would write it down.

Here is the hard part; make positive statements to off set the negative one. Sounds easy…it is not, yet if you are willing to do the work you will train yourself to become more positive. This is an exercise that is good not only for the sick people like us but for everyone. An example of this would be, if you wake up in excruciating pain…instead of telling yourself that this is going to be a real bad day, try telling yourself that you are okay and it will be a 'DO NOTHING DAY'. Realize that it will be okay, smile and relax. This too shall pass…is sometimes what I tell myself on those particular days. Try it and I bet you will feel better about yourself…that is, better as a person in this life. What do you think?

I also believe strongly in therapy, for people who are always sick need to talk to someone, yet this too is tricky for there is a lot of counselors who do not really care…they just pretend to. I have found an excellent one, a woman who has also had her hardships in life, a lady who is real, and especially a lady that cares. I can not begin to describe how she has helped me, except to say that I could not be who I am today without her.

In changing our patterns of thought, we must realize that we are living in a negative

Kathy M.

world. Just take a look around you and the evidence is everywhere, am I right? This may mean that in order to change your emotional well being, you may have to cut out the negative people in your life. This is not easy, that is for sure but if we are to survive...we must be positive. If the negative people are not people that you can stray from...get them to do the positive thought patterning with you, and if at all possible make it fun. You will find that it will bring you closer to that person.

In our lives, as sick as we are we must LEARN to keep it simple! How you may ask? By realizing that a day is just a day, another one will come tomorrow, and we can only hope that it may bring us some smiles, and maybe even some laughs!

Do not isolate yourself, as we need all the people that we can get, and if we look for them with positive attitudes, you will find they will do the same! If you are married, watch silently for a while to your partner and see if they, too, need help in their own healthy self-talk.

At first this seems impossible, yet in time it will become a natural way of life for you...and you and others around you will feel so much better, emotionally and to some degree physically, as well! You will be in control of your thoughts and therefore in control of your life!

'To hold on to negativity, keeps us stagnant...

Yet to build up our positively, opens up a whole New World!'

Kathy M.

It was due to a friend of mine, who is also a syndromite that I got a chance to look at my life in a new light. I hope it works for you as well. I asked her how she manages to get through quite well balanced as a syndromite. Her answer, so simple…yet effective. "That's the way it is," she told me. Of course, I gave her this look as if to say, "Yeah, right." Then I tried it, as I'm sure you will agree, in our desperation we will try anything that might help.

Guess what…it works, for the most part any ways, but what in life is full proof…especially ours? When you are so desperately tired, yet sleep is so far away, tell yourself, that's the way it is. When you can barely move because the pain is so bad, tell yourself…that's the way it is, and force yourself to get up anyway, even if you have to scream, that's the way it is. When you can't cook a decent supper for your family…that's the way it is! Whenever you can not be what you want because of whatever syndrome is overwhelming, well, that's the way it is!

For me this has been a miraculous tool to keep me balanced, for when I was having a good day, I felt okay but when the bad days came I would succumb to the pain and let the guilt overwhelm me…reducing me to tears. That's the way it is, seemed to balance me out with the good and the bad.

One day it became ridiculously funny to me, as I thought of my 'OWN' spot on the couch, as I'm sure you all have, as syndromites. I could not hold my laughter in, as I thought of the chalk that they use for tracing around the dead people at a crime scene. If only I could chalk out around where my body lies on the couch day after day! Can you imagine the outrageousness of a visitor finding me perfectly aligned with a chalk mark around my body on the couch? Then, I could turn to others and say, "That's the way it is!"

Instead of crying like we so desperately want to…laugh out loud as hard as you possibly can…while repeating in your mind…that's the way it is! A challenge it is but one worth taking as it can get you through those real rough days.

I remember a day when I was in a fibrofog, you know those days when you are just not with the program…I could not find the salt and pepper. After hunting high and low, asking the kids where they had put them, I found them in the refrigerator…where I had put them! Yes, that is the way it is!

'To find the laughter in the pain…
Is to find the sunshine through the rain!'

Stress…yes that unbearable word…sends not only our psyche into a whirlwind but our sickness too. It has been a long while since I have written and it is just now that I realized by reading my last words in this very book, why that is. Can you guess? Stress, of course…and yet as I read over my last chapter, I was not taking my own advice for I was not keeping it simple.

Yet, it seems as if my whole world has been turned upside down, and as I only want this to be an inspirational book, I felt that I did not have what it takes right now in my life to inspire.

What was I thinking, for although, this is a book to help others…it is also therapy and a tool for me, isn't it? For I am no different than anyone of you, as life hits us all like a brick wall that seems to get bigger and bigger, as the piles of shit get thrown at us from all directions.

In some ways maybe this is our key, to use that wall, with each individual brick containing a small part of our life. This is where we must all be STRONG…as if we are not strong enough already. For it us who built our very own walls and it us that must dig through the shit…sometimes our shovels are just not big enough!

That is why we must remember what those bricks contain, for each and every one of us has one, yet now is the time when we must look at how tall it is, how different it is.

If you think of lego it is built with its' own unique colors and sizes and although there can be fifty kids building...no two people will build exactly the same. All individuals are like that and we are the towers that keep falling down or the house with the missing piece for we are not like others, yet our walls, our inner self is strong.

As I write, I feel that we are those towers that people build just to knock down, yet no matter how scattered the pieces...we are all there. Scattered is a real good metaphor for how I have been feeling these days...can anyone relate?

For example, it is now four o'clock in the morning and I am wide-awake...what is that about? It is not like I am not tired for WE all KNOW that we are ALWAYS tired! Yet as the minutes tick by...here I sit awake. I have learned over the years not to get angry about nights like these, as there was once a time that by now I would be overwhelmed. Please, if you have not learned already, take it from me...it is much simpler to go with it than against it, after all it is just the sickness roaring its' power.

To let it aggravate you...only makes it worse, so just give in and read, write or even lay with your eyes closed...but for the love of us all...do not fight it and try to get to sleep! As we all know, when the sun comes up, we will sleep like boulders by the sea, heavy and crashing. I hope none of you reading this book live where there is twenty-four hour darkness...now that would be INSOMNIA at its' worst, what do you think?

I guess right now, I'm just trying to get a bigger shovel and even a shield as it is coming from everywhere these days...which as we all know counts me out. The stress eats away all that I have. I feel soooo tired and soooo confused, and even dizzy as I spin from pile to pile, now realizing that instead of looking at the piles, I need to look at the wall behind it, as that is where I will find my relief! WOW...I wonder which brick I need to look at. Is it small, is it in the bottom or the top, the left or the right? Which one do I start with, as I know once I start really looking, I will find the connection to the ones around it...the connection to me!

'To build a wall is what is called life...

Yet to ignore the bricks that meld the wall...

Is to ignore the power in the life we have built!'

Well…trying to keep it simple over the last few weeks has been incredibly hard and I'm sure you have all had times like these. Without going into too much detail…I will just say that life throws you wicked cards. It seems like people like you and I, are almost always dealt the hand that would fold in poker…am I right?

Nevertheless, we keep on surviving for that is what we seem to do best. In my experience, as I have told you before, one can only achieve peace when they believe in themselves…not such an easy task but very rewarding. If you follow your gut, I mean listen to your inner voice…it will tell you what you need to do. This voice is not the voice of someone else, the voice of someone sick but the voice of God.

As I have told you before, I do not attend church, yet the power of God is strong inside me. I want you all to do some homework…if you have troubles…what am I saying? When you are troubled, be silent. Go back to that wall of life and listen very carefully. Go into nature, that is, sit by a window or under a tree and concentrate only on the beauty you see. Ask for an answer to your troubled heart…then listen. Did you find your answer? It's like magic, only better, for you know the illusion and how to become the magician. You can solve the problem. This is where you must hold strong to your heart and be true to yourself…no matter what the consequences. For with God holding you in his arms, anything is possible…and those bricks of life, no matter how well built will not stop you. In fact, they will crumble beneath you as you take charge of your life. In case I have lost you, I will give you an example of how I took charge in mine.

I am a person with a huge heart, a person that will be there for everyone, or so it seems. I have always been guilty of spreading myself too thin, and believing in everyone that they are who they show themselves to be. I will not mention names, yet I will tell you that in order to take charge of my own life, I had to let others go as people such as these…no one needs in their wall of life. I'm sure you have come across people like these as well, as we all have, yet for me I must have only faith and trust in the people close to my heart.

A wall only built of these types of people cannot be built upon, as its base could never hold strong enough to put the next layer of bricks on. A wall like this can only crumble and fall…not because of church, religion or race but because of the type of mistrust that it is formed from.

Sick or not, wealthy or not, loved or not…it is only trust in yourself and the love of God that you…a human being on this earth, can possibly begin a journey of possibilities that is unique to only you in this world.

"To live your life with illness is difficult…
Yet, to live your life with misconceptions is impossible!"

To live a life of sickness is frustrating, painful, and sometimes just plain agonizing, yet what if you are the one who is NOT sick? This question raises a lot of issues for both the healthy and the ill.

There is definitely jealousy on behalf of the sick people...yes, like it or not, we have to admit it! Although we must admit this to ourselves, we do not have to live in it. For example, we must learn to let the jealousy go and concentrate on the fact that we are loved anyway! This in itself is a great gift that we have been given.

I know for me, although, I would never wish our pain on anyone, sometimes I feel if only he/she could be sick for a week...he/she would understand what it is like and what I have to go through each and every day. Do these feelings sound familiar to any of you? I'm quite sure that your answer to the above question is yes...if not you are already an extra ordinary person and should be proud of it. Yet, for the rest of us, who answered yes, we must look at the bigger picture in our life and the lives of those we love.

As I have already spoken of, I have a fiancé, and three children...my family! Since I have been ill for the entirety of my children's lives and also from the day I met my fiancé...I can only imagine how my illness has impacted their lives.

The fact that it is ongoing, never stopping and all consuming makes it a struggle for EVERYONE...not just me!

As a mother...like ALL mothers, sick or not, I only want the very best for my children, yet when I turn the tables and try to put myself in their position, I can not help but feel sad. It feels so unfair that they MUST live with a mom that is different from others. It must be hard for them to watch me suffer, and no matter what I do to try to hide those terribly bad days; they are so in tune with me...they know. It has happened so many times that tears have filled my eyes, only to be followed by tears to fill theirs. It hurts me so, for they are my children and to watch them cry makes it even harder as I know they are hurting so very deeply inside, and I so desperately want to make it okay for them.

The truth, the reality, as we already know...is that we can not just make it okay, at least entirely. The sickness is a reality, yet I have taught them that to feel angry is okay. To encourage the truth in how they feel is to encourage a way to open the door for their own acceptance.

Here again is to allow everyone...especially children...to separate our illness from ourselves as individuals. For when they are feeling angry I tell them to let it out because I know their anger is not directed at me personally, not my spirit, not my soul, not me as a mother...just the illness itself. This is hard at first because it sometimes comes out in ways that really hurt me, yet this is when I must remember to separate myself from my illness. Although, in the beginning it was hard it has become easier as the years have passed, since I have grown in understanding and confidence in who I am...on the inside, not the outside. With the inner knowledge that I have developed, it has also become easier for them to tell me exactly how they feel without me feeling hurt or angry, too. I remember telling my youngest just recently that she NEEDS to tell me her feelings and no matter what she tells me, she can not hurt my feelings or me because my illness does not represent who I am...especially as a mom. I have also learned that my children have lived in great fear and this is such a hard one to reassure them of. Actually, it is like a sword in their heart with a double-edged blade. Their fear is justified as they fear two things, that as a human being on earth, I do not KNOW that it won't become a reality for them one day, although I reassure them with ONLY positivity.

You see, my children, especially in their younger years have a real fear of my death due to my 'SICKNESS'. Although, as all those of us who are syndromites know that we will not die from this...we can not guarantee or even begin to predict when or even how we will die. We realize that being a syndromite will not lead us to death for in no way does it appear to be fatal...debilitating, without a doubt, yet not as to 'TAKE' our lives. However, not one of us knows our destiny...our time on earth...our life in it's length from beginning to end. Contrary to what I do not know about the mystery of how long I will live; I do believe that my life will be a long one, bearing pain and suffering as each day goes on. Yet bringing me stronger and closer each day to the spiritual being I long to be.

The other very real fear that they have expressed is what, I'm almost positive that any and all of our loved ones have felt at some point throughout our illness, whether vocalizing it or not is, "Will I get sick with what you have?"

This again, is another hard question to answer honestly...for however many times we pray for our loved ones to stay healthy, again there are no guarantees. It would be nice if I could predict the future for my children, yet I can not. The only thing that I CAN do is to give them the best life that I am capable of, free of abuse and full of love and understanding...then hope that God will do the rest. I do not feel that I am lying to them by telling them that their fears will not come true, I only feel confident that my love for them so strong, my wishes for them so great will bring faith to them as human beings.

It is only in this way, faith in their own inner power that they will be healthy and reassured, both in their hearts and their minds. Although every mom sometimes second-guesses herself, I feel that their reassurance is the answer that serves them best, right now anyway...at the ages of eight, nine, and ten. What do you think?

One of the hardest things for our partners, that is, love relationships, is to sit by and watch our suffering...all the time knowing that no matter what they do, they CAN NOT take our pain away.

For my sweet Eric, tries so very hard to help...and in so many ways he does, yet the frustration must be intense. He has to watch while I lye in agony...he has to watch those horrible days when the tears pour out of my very soul and into his.

For years, he too was in denial that I would get better...one day! Although, it was a comfort for him...he had to let it go, for to continue on in our REAL lives...acceptance is the only answer. Our love relationships have to be strong because living with someone who is sick is not only a challenge but also a chore. They not only have to support the family, outside the home by working, but they must take on the housework as well...at least most of it. It occurred to me just the other day, as my sickness has worsened greatly over the past year, that the reason he did not do the 'HOUSEWORK' the way I did is because he is not sick.

Let me explain...you see it took everything I had to do dishes, make a decent supper, and make lunches for the kids...so I did it simultaneously. It was not until now that I figured out why...it took ALL my energy. This was the only way I knew to get it all done. Anyway, after I became even more disabled, I would ask him why he didn't do it my way...all at once. His reply would always be the same..."Don't worry, I will get it done!" Finally...I know why he can get it done in his own way...he is not sick! He has the energy to go back and do lunches later and dishes, etc. Well, duh...was all that my mind could come up with when I came to this realization, for the only reason it makes sense to do three jobs at once...is if you were sick and it took every thing to get it done!

Anger is one of the hardest things for our loved ones to deal with, as they too, have no one to be angry at. It must be very hard to watch, as they sit helpless and watch our pain destroy us so. Although, their anger may be different...it is still justified and we must allow them to feel this way. The only solution that I have found is to literally kick them out for a while…when it has overwhelmed them to their very end. They must be able to escape from the helplessness and despair when they feel this way. It is the only thing that makes sense, for they need to be able to breathe…much as we need to be able to recognize when too much has become way too much. Communication is an absolute MUST!

Not only do our loved ones feel angry at our illness, also they can become antagonized by us, since we must face the facts…we are not easy to live with…sometimes…ha, ha, ha! We forget things we have said or done. We are up when they need to go to sleep, we get confused about dates and times and on top of all of that, we as human beings, still want to be right…especially me, as my LEO pride can be hurt very easily! Although, I think it is our human characteristic for us to want to remain in control…especially over things that we have said and done.

Let us face the facts here…they are entitled to be angry at us sometimes, for words we might have said, for the things we might have done, that we can not remember. I know how much it infuriates me when I know someone has said something and out right deny it…that is why I try…try being the key word to step back and really think about things, it's not like I don't have the time for it! Energy…well that is a whole other story but I sure do have the time.

'To allow loved ones their feelings is to let them grow...

Yet, to acknowledge them as real allows them inner strength!'

Kathy M.

Well, it has been a very long time since I have written. I feel like my life is slipping away on me...want to give something back to the world...so I guess if I wait till I'm feeling better...well, let's just say I'll never finish this book. I won't go there, though as this is a book about positivity. I'll start off by filling you in on A LOT that has happened since I last wrote. Yes more about my life...can you stand it?

Remember when I was telling you about Stress...well, that is the number one invader as it is for everyone, healthy or not. Yet in the last 6 months there has been a lot of it, some good and some bad. If you are a syndromite...you know that either takes its toll on us...am I right? As I have said before, life is so very unpredictable and to grab a little happiness is to grab the very essence of this thing called life. Where to begin is where I sit and scratch my head for so much has happened on the outside of my life that it has really thrown the inside of my life for a loop. Yet I stick to my guns and rid myself of the garbage, as one way or another...I always do. .

As I have said MANY times that my fiancé has been a wonderful support and is a wonderful man, yet he has been my fiancé for 5 years...Why you ask? He was not divorced...why... because of the custody battle over his/my son. You see his mother pushed him here...at first, but then he wanted to stay so the battle went on for years…and so did ours. I had to put my foot down and take drastic measures…such as almost splitting up with him to get him to take action. As it turned out, Scott decided to live with his mother so she finally gave Eric joint custody…meanwhile requesting that I have no contact with Scott.

Well, you have to realize that, I had become very close to him…like my own son…when I find out he too had lied to his mother about me. I don't know what he said nor do I care, the fact is that I was so very hurt. You see I have been the one who he has confided in, and I have been the one fighting for him all these years…slap, slap, slap!

This of course has caused many fights between Eric and I…as there are so many ins and outs of this story but I will save you the gory details. All that matters is Eric and I are still together and he is finally DIVORCED! We may even get married one day…who knows…ha, ha, ha!

During all of this my grandmother has become very weak and has had to go into a retirement home and we had to sell her house…the one house that I had that was stable and full of love, when I was young. This of course makes me sad, as she has had to leave her house and is very weak. She was like a mom to me for a lot of years, as was my grandpa like a father to me…GOD REST HIS

SOUL…as he has passed on. Oh, how I miss him.

Now for some good news…I finally got my disability after fighting for 8 years…and let me tell you that was a happy day! I can finally contribute to the financial well being of my family and poor Eric does not have to slave at any work he can find…just to get by. Let me tell you, that was probably one of the best days of my life, and man what a shopping spree our family had! I will let you know more about that later, for if you are like me you are probably still fighting.

Here comes the good and bad news, combined…I'll be dramatic and ask which news do you want first? Good, okay…I quit smoking cigarettes…bad…I started again. Oh my…what a roller coaster of emotions. The first week I was fine! Then suddenly as if I was hit by a tornado, I became nothing but an emotional basket case and here is the kicker, my chiropractor told me that the reason I felt awful was because ANY change in OUR system makes our body react in a flare up. Well, since it has been nothing but a flare up for months…I thought that I would persevere. After 7 weeks and still feeling horrible, especially mentally…which of course sends us into a physical frenzy…I gave up. I don't know if this is the right decision, or if I will feel any better but my thinking is that I can't feel much worse.

Then, it hit me; do we not deprive ourselves of enough? Do we not have enough day to day limitations, without adding more restrictions? Don't get me wrong...I wished I could have done it and one day I hope to, yet...I just couldn't get a handle on things and I found myself feeling that if I have to be sick any way...what is it going to hurt. I do however intend on smoking only a few a day, as when I quit...I weaned myself to 4 or 5 cigarettes a day. I felt okay with that...so back to that I go...at least for now. It just can not be my time for I was an emotional wreck...even my 8 year old daughter's reaction was a positive one, as she said, "Maybe you will stop crying now, mom!" As she said this, she said it with complete sincerity and honesty.

I'm telling you, the way I have been feeling a few days shorter on my life is not a bad thing...ha, ha,ha! It is so odd, though, for I did not even feel like myself and it is as if my old self has returned. Even though doctors won't agree and I'm sure not all who read this will agree, yet I see no harm in a few cigarettes a day...especially, if it keeps me sane...or as sane as I can be. You see I forgot that I was indeed a syndromite and no matter what I do...it rules. So do I feel bad about myself?

No...as I must like everyone as a human being...especially as syndromites we must cut ourselves a break. It is in the best interest of our well being to do what we NEED to survive day by day, and damn it if I can't do something that gives me peace of mind.

This does not mean that if you quit successfully...or are thinking of it...not to, for the LOVE OF GOD try your best...but if you do not succeed please allow yourself to accept it. It was not until I started smoking again, that I could even attempt to write again, as I could not focus. It was an experience, though, let me tell you that...I think I cried enough tears in 7 weeks to fill an entire pool...and I don't even own one...hahaha!

Although, my life has been crazy for a while and my health on a real decline...I did survive, and a little wiser, too. It was like I felt it was time to take out the garbage, you know the stuff that holds you back, keeps you stressed out, and most of which you have no control over. I have learned to let go of even more negativity and learn who I really am, and who I want to be. In one word that would be, honest...with others...and myself. It does not matter what we do, whether we overcome or succumb to life's hardships. What matters is how we feel afterwards...besides sick, of course!

"To truly love oneself in honor…
Is to be honest from the inside out!"

Let us return to the lighter side, once again, as to keep referring to the lighter side is one of our main life goals for our survival as syndromites...wouldn't you agree?

In my life experiences, I've often thought that my illness was a cruel joke but now I see that it is most certainly insane. It is at these times that it is imperative that we find the sanity inside the insanity as we look to laugh at ourselves and our circumstances!

A while ago, I was in a department store with my two daughters, in the Barbie isle as they were showing me their favorite ones. Suddenly, my legs gave way and down I went, collapsing right there between Summer Fun Barbie and Holiday Barbie.

At that moment, I was frazzled and embarrassed, wondering if I could make it out of the store. With my daughters to help...I made it out alive...but as I reflected back on the situation, I could only laugh. For they have every kind of Barbie known to mankind except...Help Me Up Barbie!

Maybe we should invent our very own Syndromite Barbie, with arms and legs that won't move; and when they do they snap and crack. She would come with a full wardrobe consisting of pajamas, a robe and fuzzy slippers. She would come with the option of knotty hair or bed head, and of course, no make-up. Syndromite Barbie would also come with accessories; a box of Kleenex, a cane, a walker, a bed and a couch. Last but not least, included would be her very own cupboard full of pills! What do you think?

Natural, herbal medicines are emerging like wild fire to help with this, that and the other...so why not syndromites, I wondered. Ginseng was the entire rave a couple of years ago...so I thought I would try it. Of course, when I asked my pharmacist, who is also a naturalpath, his reply was, "Oh no, taking that with my anti-depressants could kill me!" At that moment, I actually thought...so what? As he saw the look of distress on my face, he took me aside and recommended two other natural remedies that should help me. Here is where it gets funny!

One was in liquid form and one in tablet form...as I listened very carefully to his instructions on how to take them...or so I thought!

So off I went, hoping I might just feel a little better, trying them that night. The tablets were about as round as a dime and about a quarter inch thick and from what I remembered...remembered being the key word...I was to stick one under my tongue and let it dissolve. Let me tell you, I had that sucker in my mouth for an hour and it had only dissolved to half its original size. I couldn't talk, I could barely swallow, so after another half hour I spit it out…totally disillusioned.

The next morning, I was to take both the tablet and the liquid, so I thought I'd be smart and split the tablet in half. Well, it still would not dissolve, so once again I spit it out and in the garbage it went. Then I tried the liquid, with the directions being to mix half a teaspoon and tiny bits of water…hold it in your mouth until it dissolved! So I opened my mouth and poured it in…just as I did that my youngest daughter came into the kitchen to ask me something. There I was with my mouth full, my finger pointing to my mouth, trying to hum that I would be with her in a second. Now my daughter, still young looked at me with worry, since she had no idea what was wrong with me! I waited and I waited, as I danced around the kitchen, with my mouth full and my daughter's eyes wide with horror…it wasn't dissolving. Finally after I could no longer keep from swallowing, I spit into the sink as my daughter sat in shock, while this liquid dribbled from my mouth down my chin! After catching my breath, I was able to explain what I had been doing…imagine how funny I must have looked! After trying and trying, unsuccessfully, I finally gave up frustrated and bewildered.

It was a month later when I was refilling my prescriptions, that I again saw the pharmacist. He asked me if I was feeling any better from taking the stuff that he had given to me. I replied bluntly, "The tablets won't dissolve and neither will the liquid, so I gave up!"

He gave me a peculiar look, then said, "You chew the tablets and the natural medicines in the liquid are absorbed into your body in less than a minute, then you spit the water out, since the water won't dissolve."

"No way," was my reply, as I had to chuckle. "I've been doing it all wrong," I said, as I shook my head and laughed out loud. He was laughing with me then, as you have to admit, only a syndromite could get the directions so messed up! Just goes to show you that our life is always crazy…somehow…someway!

I have come to wonder about certain doctors…especially specialists. I wonder if they got their degree just because they were last in their class! During my syndromitis, I developed yet another syndrome, Irritable Bowel Syndrome, yet it was not the diagnosis that I found profound, rather the way he diagnosed me. I had been in excruciating pain and dropped forty pounds in two months, so as expected I was just a little worried. I sat in his office stressing my concerns and his next question was only one of insanity. "Are you under any stress?"

Kathy M.

Well, of course I am you moron! Wouldn't any one be even the slightest bit alarmed if they were dropping weight like an athlete sweats? Next, he has me lie on the table where he proceeds to stick a tube up my ass...pump me full of air...then asks if it hurts! Well, I may not be a doctor or a nurse but I can guarantee that if I stuck a tube up his ass and pumped him full of air...he would be in pain, too. What do you think? So as I return to the chair, trying ever so hard to be a lady and not fart, I wiggle about, crossing my legs, swinging side to side...he tells me that I am fine and gives me fiber tablets. He proceeds to tell me to change my diet, and stay away from...stress! I was out of there like a bolt of lightening, reaching my car, I let out a tremendous thunder of gas...and the ride home was not much better, let me tell you. That was the last time I let anything near my asshole, wouldn't you agree? Crazy as crazy can be...so it seems!

Though it may seem that I have my illnesses under control...as I have said before it was not always this way. I, too have been through a lot of ups and downs...the rollercoaster! Yet, combined with my medications I was in a twelve-week therapy group, which I found extremely helpful and empowering. Here is the punchline...they assessed my case and concluded that I was doing well, so...they kicked me out of therapy!

Imagine the thoughts running through my head! Any ways, it was after that, that I realized that I would be okay...so here I am, writing to you. Day by day, finding accomplishments in the smallest of tasks, contributing in any tiny way, trying to...stop the madness!

"To find the darkness in the madness...
Is to deprive the lightness in the goodness."

Kathy M.

It has come to my attention, as I have taken the time to think…have lots of that…for a syndromite to really feel like we are understood, first we must find someone else to relate to. As odd as this may sound, I have figured out that we, as syndromites, are like alcoholics or addicts, recovering. I realize that as you read this you may think that I have indeed finally lost my mind but as you read on I think you may very well, agree!

You see everyday…even every hour, for a person in recovery is a tremendous challenge. There are feelings of sadness, frustration, and anger and of course, questions of there own self-esteem. Does any of this sound familiar to you…as a syndromite? Even sometimes their very survival becomes a challenge, as they struggle to get through an ordinary day. Others may look down on them with a lack of understanding of what it is that they are going through. They too, like us, must feel lost, confused, and completely alone at times.

Although syndromites and people in recovery have their respective support groups, ultimately it is up to the individual to make their life a success, which as I have talked about before, can just be the ability to survive the life that we are dealt. In many cases it is the way in which one sees oneself that makes the difference in their lives, yet it is also how one deals with what they as individuals are given.

In other words, it is the perspective of which they see themselves in not only their own lives but the impact that they have on others as well.

Can you see yourself now in the eyes of a recovering alcoholic or addict? It is with great thought and humbleness that I have found this similarity, yet also with great selfishness. Let me explain, before you once again think I have gone truly insane!

People like you and I do not try to be selfish or in any way self-centered, nor do I believe recovering alcoholics or addicts wish to be…yet the way we live our lives is quite the same, almost scary. I know for myself in the past and even in the present, although we try with extreme effort to be like 'everyone else' we are not. It is an overwhelming task not to become self focused; as in everything we do, there are consequences. This is true for people recovering and syndromites alike. How do I feel today? Can I actually get through this day? I feel like a failure. Can I face my fears today? Will I get through the day without breaking down. Am I sad today? Am I frustrated today? Am I going to burst into tears today? Do I even want to see the day? Will I be strong enough today to do what I have to do? Will I have to ask for help today? All of these questions are asked to ourselves randomly, in our subconscious, as we are unaware of the tremendous toll our life takes on us. Every day is a struggle just to survive to the very next day. As we bravely cope in whatever way we can, it is our loved ones that get left in the cold…so to speak…without us even realizing it, as we do not do this on purpose, only as a survival technique.

So, it is now my goal to make a conscious effort to do less self-evaluation and more life strategies with the ones that I love. Don't get me wrong, for years I ignored my limitations and spent all my time neglecting myself to be with my children and my partner. For years, I refused to give in and kept on going as if I was a 'normal' human being…not the right decision either…as I'm sure you have all tried that one, too. The way I see it, we must each find our very own balance…that is to say whatever works for you, as an individual.

Although dealing with life in this fashion takes more of a conscious effort, I believe that it also has its benefits in our illness. You see, if we try to focus on something or someone else our pain becomes less dramatic and more tolerable, for the most part any ways…since there will always be those days, that we know about all too well. I am in no way suggesting that our pain will go away or even subside but if we can learn to ignore it, just a little bit by focusing our 'little bit' of energy on our loved ones, it may just become an annoying ache that is always there. As a result, we become more absorbed in the world around us and less absorbed in our everyday struggle. Please don't mistake me, in no way do I think or am I even suggesting that this is or ever will be easy, yet for our well being, it could be an answer.

As I have mentioned on several occasions, I am learning right along with you, my readers, our guide to survival. I do feel, however, that in finding the similarities between syndromites and recoveries', I have found an important piece to our puzzle. It is a piece that not only fits our puzzle but gives us peace of mind. What do you think?

"To find a piece of yourself by loving others...

Is to open up an inner creation of self-peace!

As time goes by, our pain worsens, it is only natural that fear sets in. Fear of what is really happening to our bodies. Fear of how long we will walk...for those of you that still can. Fear of what will go wrong next. Fear of what or who we will become. Fear of how long we have on this earth. Fear of our limitations. Fear that we will not live our life to our own satisfaction.

Yet it is with this fear that we can motivate ourselves. It is with these very fears that I write this book for I realize my time is limited. That is not to say my years are, but my time to sit at a computer and write...quite limited, I think. I have been sick since I was 18 and now at 32 have many, many more limitations. I can only write for small periods of time, which makes me realize that I have to keep my ass in gear! That is, of course, if I want to finish this book...which I feel is an absolute necessity in our society today.

Fear can be an overpowering enemy just as easily as our motivation...but only if we allow it to. Yes, we may be sick, but we still have the power of our own minds. The reason I mention this is for those of you who are afraid to the point of anxiety and panic. I used to let my fear rule me...and as I have said before, with counseling and medication...I now rule it...at least for the most part. Are you asking me if I'm scared of whether or not I will be in a wheel chair by the time I am 40? Scared as hell! Are you asking me whether or not I'm afraid I will suffer even more as the years go by? Scared as hell! However, I have chosen to challenge my fear and keep on going. Let me put it to you this way. I live my limitations. I empower myself as best as I can...I live my life whole heartedly...I try to be the best person I can be...I struggle like hell from day to day...yet fear will never get the best of me...even though it is a part of my everyday.

Panic attacks are fear of fear itself, as you have probably heard. Yet, have you heard the reason for them and what is REALLY happening to you? Since we, as syndromites, have led a life with high stress and the constant fight or flight response, as I explained earlier in this book, our body is used to pumping extra adrenaline. Adrenaline is a wonderful thing if you need it but if you are resting it becomes a not so wonderful thing. You see your body does not realize that the adrenaline is not needed and once it is pumped through the body, it starts a whirlwind of body reactions. Dizziness, nausea, trembling, heart palpitations, tunnel vision, loss of hearing, sweating, chills and of course the urge to run are all symptoms of a panic attack, or adrenaline in the body. These can make you feel as if you are having a heart attack, dying, choking, or just going crazy.

Kathy M.

What you don't realize, is that once you have the initial adrenaline flowing through your body any stress, or scary thoughts, only pump out more. Take it from me, a person who suffered for years with horrifying panic, you can beat it. All you need to do is talk yourself through it. Tell yourself that it is only Adrenaline in your body and you are having natural body reactions as a result. Accept the fact that you will be shaky and feel a little strange for a while and reassure yourself that you are okay. In fact, you are so very okay, that you are in control and will ride these body reactions out...float with them...even enjoy them...as they do give you an energy boost.

This of course, is not easy, but once you have achieved it, you will never panic again because you have handled it. Even if you do feel anxious at times, this is when you realize that the adrenaline has already been pumped and you tell yourself that you are in control. The absolute worst thing you can do is to try to fight it because as a result your body will send out more adrenaline and your anxiety will begin to escalate, along with your symptoms.

Well, how do I know you may be asking? I know because I have had them controlling my life in the past and I finally got answers on my quest for knowledge...about as easy as finding coping skills for being a syndromite...which is why I feel the need to pass on this information to you, my readers. Especially since we already have enough to deal with and overcome day by flipping day without having to battle panic, as well...don't you agree?

"To have fear that is out of control is panic...

Yet to have fear as a motivation is a life saver!'

Life as a syndromite is always one of mystery, for one never knows what the next day holds. It seems as if we cannot plan…only hope…as our life goes by. It has been one of those insomnia nights for me as I am writing in the middle of the night, although…so it seems that is when I receive the most inspiration. I finally found a word that describes my inner feelings on those bad days…emptiness. It is all consuming for it is at those times that we find it the hardest to find the lighter side, and to be honest, a lot of times…it is like trying to bottle air. You know it is there but you sure can't grasp it.

It is times like these when suicide can creep into your mind…and once it does it becomes like oxygen to a flame. Yet, we must look passed it, to the next minute, to the next hour, to the next day. Though at these times that emptiness that we feel is so very real, sinking deep into our soul that it actually hurts…at least for me.

It is at these times we must remember all that we have been through, and realize that this too shall pass. We must look at all the little things to fill that emptiness inside. We must ask God to give us the strength to hold on and for the wisdom to search for the good things in our lives.

It is my belief that if we take our own life…we will be sent back to do it all over again, and although this may or may not be true...I like to hold on to the fact that it is because that alone keeps me hanging on. It is a running joke with my girlfriends and I that we are picketing when we get to heaven...our signs will say, "WE WILL NOT GO BACK!" Every once in a while when things are going bad we come up with some real good picket lines. Can you think of any?

I feel that our emptiness can only be filled by us, and when we are feeling this way we should check how we are thinking...it is those negative bugs attacking us again, isn't it? Yet, we must not punish ourselves for letting them creep in, for they are everywhere, but we must call on our positive stampede to stamp them out! It is up to us as individuals to fight and as we have already established...we are the survivors. After all, it is the fact that we are stubborn, that we know we will win.

The important thing for all of us, I think, is to see the signs that the emptiness is coming and catch ourselves BEFORE it comes. For example, I have my kids for two weeks in a row...then they go to their dad's house. Well, as you can imagine...I am wiped out...so in comes the sickness with full force. It is then that I feel the emptiness overwhelm me from inside out, as I feel that I have no life...other than my children.

Kathy M.

I start to feel that my life is not my own…and on and on it goes, before I know it the emptiness creeps in. It is now that I must realize that my body is just repairing itself for the next 2 weeks. I must remind myself that my kids will grow older and more independent, and as they do, I can only hope that I will feel that I have more of a life of my own. So…what do I do? Hang on TIGHT…and realize that the days of emptiness will not over power you or me…!

'To feel emptiness in your very soul…
Is better than to feel nothing at all!'

Well, here I go again, only nights since the last insomniac attack! Okay, sicknesses roar your power, as I will remain calm and write my book. I must admit that I am aggravated for I am so tired...but I know that you, the readers know what I mean. Ridiculous, is all that I can say...while the minutes go by...yet Lord knows that tomorrow I will sleep like a dead person. Sometimes it scares me how deeply we sleep during the day...it is as if we were dead! Why is that? Craziness...that is for sure. I guess what I would like you to learn from this...is to go with the flow...as much as possible, of course. Although this technique is frustrating, it is a much healthier way to go about being sick...isn't that an ironic sentence...hahaha! You see, over the MANY years I have learned that to flow with it is much easier than to let it get to you. We all must face the facts, and they are that our bodies will do what our bodies will do...me must learn not to resist but find constructive ways to deal with it.

For me it is to write...you could read, knit, draw, write letters to loved ones...whatever it is chances are you will have better concentration at night, which by the way, I have never understood that either. Let us face it...we have an odd sickness but we can still use our power to outweigh its power over us. In conclusion it has not beat us for we will survive yet another night of being awake, whatever the reason may be.

Like I have said before, we cannot plan for tomorrow, as we don't know which part of the illness we will have at any given time. So, if you are having insomnia know that it is okay, and realize that the next day will be a sleep day. I realized this way back when, after my never ending battle with it, after my crash...as I call it...when I finally accepted that my body would do whatever it was going to do. It was then that I found that I needed to find something constructive to do in the middle of the night because without a focus the nights can be the hardest part to endure.

I remember before I had figured this out, it was pure hell...tossing and turning...pacing the hallway...crying...screaming inside. It is also important to remember that healthy people suffer from this condition as well. It can almost ease our pain to know this, as they have to live in the rat race and go to work the next day. We get to sleep...see how putting it into perspective can change the way you think! It is also important to know that our illness goes in cycles, sometimes never ending insomnia, sometimes never ending sleep...so in a way we balance out...or so it could seem if we look at it in this way. It is of the greatest importance that we try to stay as mentally healthy as we can, so that we are able to look at our illness in this way. As for staying mentally healthy, that is a full time job...as it always feels as if we have to be a step ahead just to get through our life...yet somehow we manage. I hope you will take this into consideration the next time that good old insomnia strikes, take a deep breathe and wait it out doing whatever it is that you enjoy doing.

God knows that during the day we have no energy for it, in fact, 95 percent of this book has been written in the wee hours of the morning. I used to think it was because I had kids but now I know that I think better at night...simply put!

'To fight a losing battle...
Is to give up on winning!'

This book would not be complete if I did not mention surviving the WEATHER! Where I live the winters are cold, yet very inconsistent. Today, it is the end of January…with regular temperatures being in the minuses, usually accompanied with wind-chill factors, making it feel like -5 at the very least. Yet today is beautiful, with the sun shining and the temperature 11 degrees.

It was as I went outside to bask in the sunlight, I realized that I felt better, yet I know as the temperature will fall…so will I. I'm not sure where you, the readers live; yet I am sure that the weather determines a lot of your days…and nights. I live near the lake, so even the summers are humid causing my health to fluctuate, yet, this is where my family is, so the thought of moving seems ridiculous to me. After all, wherever I move to there will be some kind of weather fluctuation, right?

The part that amazes me is that our bodies instinctively know what the weather is like, even when we are inside sleeping…what's up with that? For me, at least, it is the winter that seems the hardest, due to the lack of sunshine…SAD…they call it. Yet, another problem to add to the list! Whatever it is, it plays havoc with my body and my mind and this is when I find it the hardest to get through each and every day. This is when I MUST take it slow, accept my disability and most of all listen to my body. Though it is sometimes the hardest part, it is when I must do my positive self-talk...and look on the lighter side. Do you agree? It is at these challenging times that we must become our own best friend and be easier on ourselves. If there are days when we just can't do anything, we must remember that we are doing the most important thing by doing this.... Resting!

By doing this, we are in fact choosing to help ourselves through the hard times, no matter how frustrating and ridiculous they may seem. As we think logically though, don't we deserve to do right by ourselves?

Even if it is one of the most beautiful days outside, it may be one of the worst for our insides; we may be in agony! I used to...and sometimes still do...have a hard time accepting my limitations on these days, as just like everyone else, I am human, and it feels like I'm stagnant, watching the world go by...without me. Are you relating to me?

An answer that I have found to this problem, is actually quite a simple one...as we must remember to keep it simple. Even if I can't get dressed, I put on my robe and slippers and hobble outside to sit in the chair on my porch. You see I do not care if my hair is brushed, or if my neighbors see me this way, it only matters that I am taking care of myself. Actually, I'd be willing to bet that each and every one of my neighbors knows what my robe looks like! This is again is a step in self-acceptance, for you or I have nothing to prove to the outside world, it is ourselves that we must take care of.

So for today, at least right now, I feel good, yet I instinctively prepare myself emotionally for the fall that is to come, when the weather, once again returns to winter at its usual. This is not to say that I am intentionally expecting to feel bad within the next few days but I have been a syndromite long enough to be realistic.

Healthy people may say that you are choosing to be sick because of this thinking pattern, for to them it is not realistic…yet we live our reality and therefore we must try to be one step ahead to prepare for the inevitable. That is fact…that is our life. Does this mean that we waste our good days, waiting for the bad ones? Of course not, yet we have to be real both for our mental health and our physical survival. Wouldn't you agree?

Sunshine is a healer for a syndromite, any way you look at it…so even if you can't hobble outside, open up your curtains, lay on the couch, or even in your bed, and feel the heat of the sunshine warm your body from your head down to your toes. For me it is a sensation that can not even be put into words accept to say aahh!

The weather and all its variations can actually be a paradox to us, as syndromites. For although it is supposed to follow certain patterns...Mother Nature certainly does not. Trained professionals who have chosen to study weather patterns for their life career can no more predict what Mother Nature will do day after day, just as we can no more predict what we will feel like day after day. A coincidence it may be or are we somehow, on some level connected to Mother Nature, herself. What an awesome thought!

"To be prepared for the ups and downs...
Is to be healthy in body and mind!"

Kathy M.

As human beings we are also sexual beings, as well. This is one area of our illness that can be very hard both mentally and physically. You may think that this is not of importance...as being ill we have so many other obstacles to overcome...why worry about that part of ourselves...to add even more confusion. Here is why I think that this issue must be looked at in greater depth. First, like I have already mentioned, WE ARE sexual beings. Second, I believe that to be a whole person, one must truly get to know one-self on an intimate level. Third, to have a relationship with another person on an intimate level, sex is an important factor...not just for the act itself but the closeness it brings to you and your partner. Fourth, we as sufferers need to realize that we are disabled and may be different in this area, as do are significant others. I will go into more detail in the next few paragraphs...as I am sure, once again you will relate.

Although none of us walk around with our illness, relating it to sex, we do need to realize that it is a human instinct to want and enjoy sexual relations. It is a natural desire that we have been given as human beings, and as I am a very sexual woman, I know that our illness infects yet another area of our lives...even if the desire is there, the physical ability is often at risk.

To truly know your whole self, sick or not, you must look inside yourself on a sexual level, as well. Since it is in fact our instinct, you must allow yourself the freedom of intimacy towards yourself…as this is an integral part of what makes you who you are. Please let me explain that it is not the physical aspect of your sexuality as much as it is the emotional part of your mind. For example, someone who knows themselves on an intimate level will feel comfortable being themselves, both alone or with others. To know your deep desires is to help yourself in understanding your emotions, both past and present.

This allows you the freedom of being yourself and how you as an individual handle the intimate details in your life. It gives you the gift of choice when you truly become on an intimate level with yourself. Have I lost you yet?

Say, for example you have two babies, both as we already know made up of completely unique genes. As they grow up, people of the opposite sex sexually abuse one child. Remembering the definition of abuse that I used before, the other child is over protected and sheltered from life.

Here we have completely different values that are being instilled in two different children…yet both potentially dangerous. It is only when they grow more mature and get in touch with their OWN intimate side, that they will choose their sexuality…one that is right for them. How does this relate to syndromites? Remember that the one thing that all syndromites start off with is abuse…in one form or another, as I explained earlier in this book. Will that mean that both these babies are headed to become one of us…no…but the danger is there, as is the potential. No one is to say how these two grown people will react to their given lives.

Yet, to say that the first of the adults may feel certain closeness to the same sex is a very possible reality…both mentally and physically. To say that the second of the adults may become quite promiscuous and a little on the wild side is also a very real possibility…as it is a way to take control of not having any more to do with that sheltered life. As they grow to be more intimate with themselves, they will know what truly makes them happy…on the inside. This is essential for us, as syndromites, as to have control over our lives is almost impossible, yet to have control over our sexuality makes us whole.

Since we are syndromites…let's be realistic…we enjoy sex as much as the next person does but we pay the cost! That is to say that we want the intimacy in our relationship yet to physically have it is sometimes just not possible. This is sometimes very hard on a relationship, but even more so on you...if you allow the illness its power. To be a person that pain is ALWAYS a part of your life is hard and sex, as physical as it is, is not easy.

However, to let the pain get in the way of your intimacy with another...is to let it beat you. This is not to say that you should be a walking sex maniac...but to let the illness control every aspect of that part of you is to give in to it. Sometimes the saying, "No pain, no gain," plays an important part in our sex lives, as syndromites. It is important for any relationship to have its own intimacy and even if you may pay the cost tomorrow, sometimes it is worth the price today.

This of course, depends on how much of a syndromite you are; yet there are ways to keep intimacy in your relationship, regardless. This is not only a human need but also a necessity, for your partner...but mostly for you. We already have so much that we HAVE to give up, we must be fair to ourselves in knowing that this part of our lives we can NEVER give up. Without intimacy in a relationship there is a lack of closeness, the closeness that makes a relationship different from a friendship. Don't you agree?

On the other side of the coin, we have the partner, who knows the pain that you endure, yet is also a human being with a sexual side. It is important for them to be able to express their own intimacy and share it with you. This is where it is absolutely essential for them to value you as a person first, then as a syndromite. If your significant other does not understand the cost that we pay…it is a must that you explain…in great detail if needed! They must learn to accept this and not push beyond the limits, however they also need to be allowed their own set of feelings.

I would call this the balance of intimacy in a relationship…and as with all aspects of life…there must be one!

In my life, with my partner, it has been like a rollercoaster in finding our balance of intimacy. At first, my illness was not as bad, and like I said before, I am a very sexual woman. However, the years have passed, as my illness has worsened, and it became more difficult to maintain that kind of a sex life.

Eric is an understanding man and realizing that my challenges were more, after a time he stopped attempting to have a sex life. This is of course, was not what he wanted but thought that it was what I needed.

There, we had it…a complete lack of intimacy between us. As I began to feel farther out of touch with him and him with me, our relationship started to get tough. It was during this rough spot that I realized we needed our intimacy back…even if I was in pain. So as the time passed, we have found our balance, and have realized our need to be close to one another. This does not mean in any way that it is easy for either one of us, as our times together are not all that much but cherished dearly.

Once again, an obstacle for a syndromite to overcome, yet, I'm living proof that the illness does not have to win!

Quickly, I will turn to the lighter side, for even though this is personal…it is funny. It was in the middle of hot and heavy sex when…I shrieked in pain as both of my legs, simultaneously, cramped up! We stopped for awhile, and after it passed, we continued our rendezvous until…he jumped off the bed, grabbing at his leg that had now cramped up! Well, if that was not enough to send us both rolling on the bed, roaring in laughter…after his leg was better, of course!

Even as I write this, I can not stop a smile from coming to my face, as it was like something off of funniest home videos…rated triple x, of course.

'To have intimacy in your life and love…
Is to have freedom within yourself!'

To maintain freedom within yourself, when you are ill, is a challenge...but not impossible. This is where you must remember to believe in yourself and who you are. You must step out of the sick label and walk into the room of wellness...mental wellness!

To be able to do this it is essential to know who you are as a person, not defined by your illness. For example, if you picture a gateway in front of you and you are standing naked before it. As you walk through the gateway you become embraced with loving thoughts and clothed in elegance. For you see on the other side of the gateway, there is the grace and beauty, like a meadow of daisies, you are transformed. You are proud and content to be who you are, just the way you are. Others see you in awe, and are jealous of your inner beauty...your inner self. Your confidence exudes you and you are in your ultimate element.

To picture this inside your head seems so easy but your asking...how to actually be that person, right? The only answer to that question is a simple one. Grow to know your inner self and love that person unconditionally. This of course, is not easy...but well worth the time and effort. If you are not sure who you are, you must find out...this is an absolute necessity. How? There are many ways, some of which I have already described and some that I will explain a little now.

It is absolutely crucial, to look on the positive side, as this word is actually your key to self-wisdom. Though, you are sick, if you find the things about yourself that you are truly grateful for you will find the true essence of your being. You must look inside to find that key...you see that is the key that holds your freedom, and then, and only then, can you walk through that gateway to the other side. Close your eyes and think about where that key is hiding...if only for a moment.

Chances are that key is complex, held both in your heart and in your mind, yet when combined together, you will find it is hidden in your mind. Feelings of inadequacy come into play when you are physically ill, yet you must release the key from your mind, knowing, without a shadow of a doubt, that you are a complete human being and you deserve to feel like one...no matter how sick you may be.

Being ill has not taken your heart away, nor has it taken you away. You must learn to be proud of who you are and love yourself completely. This is no easy task...even for the healthy...yet it is because we are ill that we get the chance to stop and get to know the real us.

Since we have to struggle so very hard in our lives, we also get to find out what makes us feel good and what makes us feel bad. What is it that you treasure? What is it that makes you sad? What is it that gets you up everyday...to face another one? These are the things that will get you to find that key...although it may be very deep. However, like I have said before, we just may be the most deep, compassionate people on this earth...for struggle and pain are our middle names! We know pain, and we can help others through theirs, and that is what we were put here for, is it not?

You may wonder why we have to look so deep...because in order to get sick in the first place means that we have buried crucial parts of our lives inside of us. Why? Pain of course, for it is hard to face those skeletons in our closets, yet whether this makes you happy or not, it must be done. I am still finding skeletons...and believe me...they hurt...but once I let them out, I can deal with them. Once I deal with them, one by one, I can let them go...not just for a while...for good. A great method for me is to write to who ever it concerns, tell them that they cannot hurt me anymore and say goodbye. There are some people that you may want to send letters to, or burn them and as you watch them burn on the paper...a little piece of your heart comes back. By doing this you have regained your power...and they cannot hurt you anymore. For even in a fleeting moment if they pass by your thoughts...you feel empowered...and there will be no more pain.

Once again, you have bettered yourself by not only getting rid of their memory, but you have also taken the route of forgiveness, and without that...anger holds your key.

Although, I go on to blab about looking deep inside...I know how very hard this is. It is now that I will let you in on how I overcame and walked proudly through those gates and into the daisies, yet don't get me wrong, there are still times when I must be pushed through that gateway. By who you might ask...by my self, as hard as it still is I refuse to stay in the meadow of darkness and dried up daisies.

Through the years, I have found some wonderful techniques to give me that push and now I will share. Healthy self-talk, as I have mentioned before is critical. You must learn to know that you are worth it. Try writing down what you think others...friends...family...loved ones, see when they look at you. Here it is very tricky, for you must stay in the positive...for example, my loved ones see me as humorous, honest and compassionate. Although I am sick that is not what they see. What qualities do you hold as a person...again write them down. Ask your friends and family to write the "GOOD" things that they see in you. Here is where you must be totally honest with yourself.

Stop the guilt, stop the "I can only do's"...stop the negativity! I know...yes but! No, there are only yes...no buts! Stop worrying about what others think and start concentrating on the facts. Stop the guilt for being who you are...for although you are sick, you are still a good person. Stop being angry, and turn it into positive energy...energy that will build your confidence. For example, if someone says something that puts you down, turn the other cheek and walk away proud...for people who put you down are not worth your time or energy. Take time for yourself...love yourself...you deserve it.

Learn to be assertive and tell people how you feel...this is tricky for you can easily become aggressive. It is essential that you keep accusations out and take responsibility for your own feelings. For example...I feel that I deserve a little more respect for what I manage to do, day by day, even when I am struggling day by day to survive. Along my path, since I have become assertive, I have found much success in dealing with how I really feel and expressing myself positively. As a result, I have less anger and more control over how I feel.

Practice high lights and low lights, as a daily ritual. This is to find at least 1 good thing that happened in your day...and 1 not so nice thing that happened in your day. Try to see if you can find more high lights than low lights.

Keep a journal, and write everything down...reread in a week and circle all the negative thoughts you have had in this time. Try to replace them with good qualities, for all negative ones are lies.

What are your expectations of yourself? Are you being realistic? Write down 10 expectations that you have about yourself? Are they obtainable? If you are anything like I was when I did this exercise, they will be just slightly ridiculous, and not achievable. You are only one person...that is something you might want to recheck every so often...for it seems so easy to expect way too much from yourself! This is self abuse and a set up for you to feel like a failure! It is possible to go through all of this on your own but my advice is to find a good counselor to help you through...as I have told you before...mine has helped me to get where I am today.

LOVE is one of the strongest and most powerful things to be able to believe in you. I've often asked Eric, why he loves me. What a question, don't you think? His answer has always remained the same...because you are you. I'll bet that if you asked a loved one this question they will say the same. So if they love you for you, wouldn't that be the logical thing for you to start doing. Tell yourself you love yourself every single day...this is important, for as we all know that if you hear something, enough…you start to believe it. You will start to believe in YOU!

One of the most important things is to surround you with friend's…true friends…and remember it is not the quantity of friends, it is the quality of them. Make sure you have good listeners around you, people that will give you a Kleenex on those miserable days…that we all know so well. People who will listen to the same sobs over and over and let you release, cry on their shoulder…and never underestimate what a hug can do for you.

Write a list of all the things and people you have to be grateful for and turn to this list often…you may be surprised at how very long that list is…I know that I was.

'To question the lies and find the truth in you…

Is to find love, pride, strength and forgiveness!'

Here I sit, once again in the wee hours of the morning...what's up, I ask myself. The answer is a simple one...me! Why, you ask? I don't have the slightest idea...can you relate? So here I go attempting to take the lighter side...join me, won't you? Let's have some fun.

I'd like to take the chance now to let you in on a secret. I am a member of the FBI, that is, Faulty.Bedtime.Institute. I am also a member of the CIA, that is, Chronically.Ill.Affilliation. There have been times when I have wanted to be a part of the PTO, yet I just couldn't be a Psychological. Test. Official. I am without a doubt a MOM, Mind out of Memory, belonging to the IRS, you know, the Inexplicable.Rash.Sightings. My house is usually LTD, Literal Tornado Disaster. By now you know that I am part of I.N.C, Inevitable Nocturnal Creatures. I also feel that I am a part of my fiancé's company, E.T.I., for I am an Extremely Tired Individual. I do have D.V.D.'s, which is due to the Diarrhea in Varying Degrees. In my own body I actually am AOL, Absent On Leave. VCR is a must since there is Virtual Chaos Regularly.

It is a necessity that I have a CB ready at all times, for a syndromite without a Couch or Bed is SOL...shit out of luck! Did you know that until recently those were my license plate letters, all kidding aside...that is the truth!

Kathy M.

Although I try so very hard to avoid it, as a syndromite, I am a SAINT...So Absolutely, Insanely, Needlessly Tired. As we suffer, we become COPS, Confused Over Pill Sequence, at least I know that I do. My cat is on steroids for his back injury and one of these days, I'm sure I will give him one of my sleeping pills. Imagine! We might mistake him for being in a coma!

Our lives sure are not the norm, yet I hope I am showing you ways to make it a little brighter along your path. Try having some fun with abbreviations, after all what else do we have to do? In the meantime, you may be thinking that I am one WWW, a Wacky, Weird Woman...and I'd have to say that you are right!

'To find ways of coping as a syndromite...
Only makes it a lot more fun to get through each day!'

This book I write in truth, so here I go, not on the lighter side. Today and tonight I sit in great pain, wondering where it's all going. Hang on…is all I can seem to say to myself. The pain is through every inch of my body and it is SCREAMING. I felt as if I must write, even though, I am writing on the lighter side. I did not want this to be depressing…but I do want to be truthful.

If I leave my times like this completely out, then how truth based can it be for others like me? To be honest, right now…I want out of this wretched pain and death seems like a good thing…although I realize this is not a solution. Yet, how do you take days and days of pain, and always look at the bright side? I am not God and I do not know that answer. Right now all I know are tears and pain. It scares the hell out of me to think that I am only 32 and already, the days of freedom are becoming more and more limited. When I say freedom, I only mean the better days…yet they are coming less and less.

More and more I am feeling trapped like a prisoner in my own body, and as that prisoner I feel wrongly accused. I feel cheated out of life, a real one that is and I feel sadness that overwhelms me, as I struggle to hang on to see any of the lighter side. I can not explain to you the pain…but you already know it. I can not describe the anger…as you already know it. I can only explain how I feel bombarded in every sense of the word.

My body feels like it is fighting a war that is not there and my emotions are sadness and grief. I am sad because I can never do the things in life that I want to be able to, and I am grieving for that person who has disappeared. My own words of wisdom are running through my head, yet for whatever the reason...right now I can't find any to justify my pain.

I feel as if my boundaries have become smaller and to be honest, I'm afraid of just how small they might get in my future. Right now, I feel like am being punished, yet I know this holds no truth. Yet if I don't allow myself to have my own feelings...I am putting more boundaries on myself. I knew I had to write, yet I'm not sure why as of yet, but my readers do need to know the reality of my life, too.

So as I write, I wonder how to find the lighter side myself. Acceptance may be the key. Loving myself may be the other key. Yet I have to ask where is the door that will fit these keys. I guess that is my question. At this time the only door is to my mind, for my heart aches to be free. So I must take this key and open the door in my mind?

In my thoughts I can hear what is on the other side of that door. Can you guess what is on the other side? Yes, the lighter side...the side where the other Kathy sits waiting patiently for me to open it up. The problem is…the door seems so big and heavy right now. I am exhausted, my energy drained and my pain giving way to tears. As I sit quietly, I can hear her thoughts on the other side. It is just a bad time right now…this too shall pass. Hesitation holds me back, yet I am not sure why.

Right now, I guess I'm tired of the fight to survive. I'm tired of the pain and the living life without really living it, and I know all of you know what I mean by that. I'm tired of struggling with life and all its stress, while at the same time struggling through my day to day suffering.

I feel rebellion when I hear that other Kathy so eager to tell me to look on the lighter side, yet I know that is my only escape. I know that other Kathy very well and she is the one who keeps me going, and through it all I realize that other Kathy is working through the voice of God, yet I cannot help but to feel anger.

As I go to that door, I hear the answer for me right now. I must give myself a break. I must listen to my body and get rest. How is my question? As we all know, life does not stop for us. So as I listen to the other thoughts…it is now that I realize that I do need to take a break. As I take the key to open the door…I put the key in its lock ever so slowly, and nudge it reluctantly.

What do I find? I find that lighter side Kathy, her arms open wide with a smile on her face. She hugs me tight, and in her warm embrace I can feel the warmth of understanding. In God's presence...I feel love, like I always do. You see it is okay to not want to be a part of the lighter side, all the time. The words are rushing through me now, "Give yourself a break, treat yourself with kindness and love. You do not always have to feel the lighter side to live it...just to let it in, is enough." I wonder now, if any of you readers understand this. Are you?

You see, when I sat down to write, I knew it was God who was telling me to, yet I did not understand why...for all I felt was pain and sorrow. What good would it do my readers to hear me cry the blues? With an urge that would not go away...I sat down, having no clue as to what words I would write, yet I knew that is what I must do. Now I realize that this was the only way for me to get back to the lighter side. You see, writing is a gift that God gave to me and I believe I am to reach out to others with it. I hope and pray that you got some clearer understanding out of me writing, and I can only dream that you will take this as a sign for you to listen...even when you thought you had listened enough.

Since I have sat down to write tonight I feel an underlying wellness. A feeling that I can once again endure whatever comes my way and a feeling of relief that I am allowed to have a break. I feel as though I will be okay. I just need some tender loving care, and it is only me who can allow that to happen. Can you? Will you?

'Giving up is not an option...
Yet, giving in is a necessity!'

If there was a record setting book for syndromites, can you imagine the events that would be listed? As it stands we probably could be in the Guinness Book of World Records!

The categories could include all kinds of insane competitions. Who could sleep the longest? Who had the longest bout of insomnia? Who could be the person that went to the doctor's the most in one month…that one would be a close one. Who would judge our events, as no one could remember long enough!

Are you laughing yet? We could have our very own Olympics, yet some of us would forget the time, some of us would forget the date, some of us would set out to come, only to forget where they were going!

We could have a competition on who has been constipated the longest, who has had diarrhea the longest, and of course, disgusting but important…who's shit is the longest. That always blows my mind, when I see that shit completely curl to fill the toilet…that came out of me? Irritable Bowel…I GUESS!

We could enter lists of medication, which one takes the most, who has the most side effects, and who takes the medications with the most colors. I've had an ongoing joke with another syndromite about a rainbow pill…wouldn't that be pretty?

Although we could not measure pain as a rule…we could videotape ourselves getting up in the morning, of course it could be afternoon or night as well. We could see who takes the longest to actually get out of bed, who takes the longest to get up, and who takes the longest to walk to the bathroom for that wake up pee. We could even have a competition for who has actually peed in their bed the most, and of course let's not forget peed while trying to get to the bathroom!

We could have walking races, for the longest distance before your body does that objection thing. We could have cane races and wheel chair races. We could see who could stand the longest, who could sit the longest and who could lie down the longest. The latter one would be a heck of a competition, don't you think?

We could do synchronized crying, crawling, stumbling, and sighing. Have you ever noticed how much that you sigh? If not, pay attention to yourself, I guarantee that you will be amazed. I know that I was when someone pointed it out to me. I find my oldest daughter has picked that up from me...oh well, that is life with a syndromite. In fact, I have noticed how much I moan when I sit or lie down. It is like an instant release that my body gives out. Stranger than fiction...that is us!

Yet if we can find ways...any way...of putting our life in perspective with a little strategy, combined with humor...that is our link to survival. You see, physically I am no better than the last time I wrote, yet I knew that it was time to throw some humor in...not only in my writing but in my life, too.

I find that the lighter side is ALWAYS there, yet a lot of the times it is like an adventure hunt to find it. Just minutes ago, I was racking my brain trying to find some humor to get back to the lighter side. Sometimes you have to look at the things you can not do, to find the insane things to think about to keep you on the lighter side.

Ah, I just thought of another competition...who has the most phlegm balls in a week's time. Who goes through the most Kleenex on a day to day schedule? Who has the longest standing sore throat, and who has the most swollen glands at one time?

Who has gone the longest without showering...due to pure exhaustion, of course? Who has worn the same pajamas for the longest consecutive days in a row? Who has not ventured out of their house for the most consecutive days in a row?

Can you imagine what all of these things would entail, and truly insane we would look? Yet, only you and I know that these could be real races, competitions and events! No, it does not mean we are crazy, only trying to find the lighter side in our lives. Everyone living in this world today, should only be so lucky as to find humor in their pain, yet that is why we are special people...wouldn't you agree?

'To let your mind wander into the lighter side...
Allows you to take back your control in your life!'

Kathy M.

Sometimes in life we have to put things in perspective, especially syndromites, such as us. Life seems to take control of us, like a chair being pulled out from under us. As of yet, I have no real answers to this...as life is basically one struggle after another, both for the healthy and the ill.

It is the stress of life that holds us back, though...no matter which way we look at it. It is now that I will give you my advice about disability. Whatever you do...don't give up! Even though I went through an incredibly long fight...it was worth it in the end. Do not allow them to break your spirit, for that is what they are trying to do. You are worth it! You deserve to be treated financially, as you are sick.

It is absolutely essential, however, no matter what they may say to get a lawyer first thing. It is normal for the first denial, for that is their process, yet after that, without a lawyer...you may be looking at a long haul, as I did. When I finally got a lawyer, they settled without a trial. Believe that one!

It is of my opinion that they treat us as numbers on a list...and if your number comes up denied...you are screwed. I did not feel I needed disability to live off the government, I felt that I needed disability in fairness to my family and me. I needed to be validated first of all...and secondly, I needed to know that I could contribute to the financial well being of my family. As we all know how useless we sometimes feel in every other area of our lives.

I wish I could tell you that I could change the system...but I can tell you to fight, fight, and fight. I must admit after my last denial, I was ready to give up...for after all I was sick. I was not only sick of being sick, I was sick of the fight. Yet as I have said before, we are stronger than we know ourselves...and somewhere we can find that little bit of energy to fight for ourselves.

In fact that little bit of energy is what keeps us surviving day by day...it is our strength, our inner spirit that will in the end keep us alive and beat them at their own game.

You see, I believe that is what the people that run disability are doing...playing their own game...only they don't play by the rules...they make them up as they go along! Yet, it is very important that you don't play their game.

Do not let them roll the dice...you roll them. Take control and let them know that you are not going away...no matter what! In the end they will give in and give up...as in any game someone gets bored after awhile...make it be them, not you! Believe me, I know the frustration and especially the anger that they provoke inside...which is stress...yet a necessary one for you to persevere. Know that, somehow, someday, you will break them down and they will toss in their dice...to you.

I cannot stress the importance of a lawyer...one who deals with fighting for disability cases. As I know that if I had not had one, I too would have been denied for the final time. The waiting game is another of their favorites. I remember one of my last letters stated that due to the number of cases at this level it would be at least a year before I heard a word...and that was with a lawyer, and only to have a hearing date!

So my biggest question is, as yours, how come there are SO many cases at THIS level. You would think that would tell them something, yet we are talking about the government here! No, I'm not bitter at all...what do you think?

The main thing I wish to relate to my readers is that you are worth it and never under estimate yourself, especially financially. Due to the stress that we have financially...it makes our lives even harder...as if we need that. I'm not suggesting in any way that money can replace bad health, yet it can make it just a little more bearable to survival each and every day, both physically and emotionally.

I know that I can speak for us all...we would give up our financial status, whatever that may be...to be healthy again, at least I know that I would.

Finally, do not let them talk down to you, or make you feel that you are any less of a person because you need help from them. Remember who you are as a human being and do not let them reduce you to that number that they so desperately want you to be. Stand straight, stand strong and believe in yourself. This is something that you deserve after having no choice in becoming ill. Let them hear the real you...and don't be afraid to let them know that you have nothing to be ashamed of. It is your right as a human being to be treated like one.

When they ask you for more medical information...demand that they be specific, for it was not until my lawyer handled my case that they contacted my doctor for specific results to specific tests. One test that I know for sure is a blood test to measure your cortisol levels in your blood...and another is a muscle weakness test...very painful but effective for disability.

I feel that I owe my doctor the world and my lawyer too for without them...I would still be without an income of my own. Doctors are also a very important part to winning your disability trial, for they must be behind you 100 percent. Be very careful, though, for one screwy report from a doctor will give them even more reason to question your authenticity.

Co-operation is another huge aspect to qualifying in all of their disability terms. Basically, you must oblige and see any doctors they request, no matter how crazy they may be.

Answer their questions honestly and openly for you have nothing to hide.

I had to see a doctor that told me that before I left his office, I would be able to touch my toes. He then argued with me about my height until he finally measured me to his satisfaction. He had his wife come down, while she sat on a table and did stretches that he wanted to teach me to do, he ever so casually told me that she was hypnotized the whole time. He stretched me and bent me and pulled me, and if that was not enough, he spun my foot around the opposite direction and asked me if it hurt!

Needless to say when I left, I knew I would never go back...yet it was for disability. I stayed through literal torture, and could not move due to pain for three days! Crazy...I'd say!

'To suffer without validation financially...
Is to suffer without believing in yourself!'

Be careful what you wish for! I say this with prior knowledge of some sort. It was not even a year ago when I went to the doctor and told her that my irritable bladder was getting worse. I had sudden urgencies to go, with absolutely no warning ahead of time. I was sometimes peeing in my bed, as I could not make it to the bathroom.

A look of concern came to my doctor's face, as she told me that she must check for bladder infection. I took this in stride as over the years, I have had several of these...in fact, many times diagnosing myself to the doctor. When the test turned up negative for infection, she told me that I must go for an ultrasound.

As we all know, this is like going for a haircut for us...as there is no big deal...due to the fact that there is never anything wrong. So off to the ultrasound I went...full of water...ready to explode at anytime. For those of you who have not had a pelvic ultrasound lately, they now have a tool...looks like a big dildo...that they stick inside.

Alrighty then! I was thinking to myself, as I emptied my bladder for this new and improved gadget that would let them take a closer look around. Ha, ha... I had to chuckle just a little when she slipped a condom over it for protection! So after what I would call an interesting afternoon, I went home with not a worry in my head…as I already knew there would be nothing to see.

It was 2 days later, when I got a phone call from the doctors office that my jaw dropped to the floor…she wanted to see me as soon as possible. Fear came over me then, as I realized that there must be something wrong, although it was minor since I just knew it would be some little problem.

As I sat and listened to her tell me that there was an eight by five-centimeter mass on my right ovary and she was sending me to the gynecologist immediately…I was still very calm. She explained that with the ultrasound they could not tell what the mass was but the gynecologist would be able to tell me more. It could be cancer, she told me with a great look of sadness on her face. Still, I remained calm…like it was all a dream…since whatever was wrong with me had to be some sort of syndrome that no one could do anything about…but it would not kill me!

It was at the gynecologist's office that the fear came rushing inside me. He was a very kind man and very honest. He told me that I would need surgery as soon as possible and that he would be putting me on the emergency list. He told me that the only way to know what they were dealing with was to go inside…the worst case scenario…a complete hysterectomy, if there was cancer and any sign that it had spread.

He checked me internally, quickly but thoroughly, then said that it felt like it had shrunk from the size of the previous ultrasound. He decided to send me for another one, just to be thorough and know what he was looking at before the surgery.

It was not until the night before that I went back to see him, that I completely lost it. All I kept thinking was that I did this to myself because I had always wished for something to take me away from this pain. I remember praying to God a million times over, asking him to just take me, that I wanted out of this life of pain. It was that night that I realized that I was not ready to die yet, no matter how bad the pain. I have children, a husband-to-be, parents, and friends. Oh, how I wanted to take back all those wishes from before, yet I couldn't...could I?

When I returned for the results the next day, he had a wonderful smile on his face. Caught off guard, I took a seat and waited for his words, barely breathing. "It has disappeared," he said cheerfully. Before I sighed, a sigh of relief he had to tell me again, as I was in total disbelief. He went on to tell me that it must have been a really large cyst on my ovary and that it is very common for them to come and go.

Thank you God, is all I could think as I left the office with a smile ear to ear. It was the power of prayer that I am sure of, as all of my family and friends had been praying for me. It was also my wake up call...my reality checks...I wanted to live!

I hope my story has touched your hearts, yet also helped you to realize that to wish for something that you might not want is not a good idea. Don't get me wrong, I still have those days where I feel like I want out but my thoughts quickly return to my very real experience, and somehow I find the strength to carry on. So will you!

Almost being a victim of cancer has made my heart and soul fall open to all those who have not been as lucky as I. To those who have suffered through the battle, and to those who lost the battle...my best wishes and heartfelt sorrows are with you all. My own dear grandpa died to that battle and not a day goes by that I do not remember him.

So, for all of you syndromites, in some ways be thankful...for we still have the chance to see another day...no matter what that day will bring. That in itself, is a true gift...so be very careful what you wish for!

'To wish to be free of pain is healthy...
Yet to wish to be free of life is cowardly!'

Money is just one of those things that is almost always a stress, for the healthy and the ill. I know that throughout my entire life, it has been for me...yet it must be put in perspective.

It was only two Saturdays ago, when I sat up all night in the emergency, watching my youngest daughter, so little and helpless in the emergency room bed. She had possible appendicitis...so with an Intravenous in her tiny little wrist...we waited to see if it was just a bladder infection. By morning they would know as they were giving her antibiotics through her IV. As I sat by her side, horrified that she may need surgery, I talked to God over and over, pleading for her...it became clear to me then.

For as long as I have known I have worried about money, but what is money anyway? It can not buy you love...or good health. It was that very long night in emergency that I vowed that I would no longer let money worries be more important. This was my own baby in that bed and all the money in the world could not buy her health on that night.

Luckily...thank you, God...it was just a severe bladder infection, and with a prescription we were on our way home by 10 o`clock the next morning.

This served as a great lesson for me, as money will come and money will go, yet the people we love are what are really important,

Kathy M.

for no money can change their fate. I am not saying that money should be spent frivolously, or not shed a concern…for we all have to be responsible.

However, as a person with never enough money…so it seems…as most of the world can relate, it must be put into perspective, especially for the ill, as we are. As we already know what stress does to our health, let us not allow money to be such a powerful trigger.

It has been said that you can not get blood from a stone, nor can you get money from worry. In our lives we must concentrate on the things that we have control over and let the rest go. Trust me when I say that it is not easy for me to live this way either, yet since that incident whenever a money concern comes to mind…all I can picture is my precious daughter lying in that hospital bed. It changes my perspective and I think…no matter what crisis comes…where there is a will there is a way, when money is concerned.

Let us not forget about our God, as we may all of a sudden receive money that we never counted on, or a surprise gift in the form of money. Let it go…give it to Him, as he is the only one who can really control it anyway. Do you agree?

'In our life we have so many controlling issues...

Let us not allow money issues to control us, too!'

Although, I am writing this book for the ill…I do want you to realize that I am the ill, as well. It has taken me several years to write this book and many a day where I have had to push myself to do so. Sometimes the push has come from pure determination and sometimes it has come from the fear of getting it finished before I may not be able to. Yet, there has ALWAYS been a push from God, or my inner self, whichever way you want to see it. I believe that I am supposed to help others, as we all are, and this is my way of doing so.

I find myself coming near the end of my words of wisdom…if that is what they are, so now I feel that it is time to tell you my recommendations…how I survive, day by day…besides what I have already written. These are not things that you must do, however in my long experience as a syndromite, they have gotten me through.

Natural health remedies have helped some people that I know, yet for me, I never found much of a difference. I take a multivitamin with minerals and a stress vitamin B complex with extra vitamin C and Iron, not just once a day but twice. Apparently, people with our problems are strongly lacking in their B vitamins, and we need all the multivitamins we can get. Whatever you do…don't take too much iron…irritable bowel…look out!

I have found that Celebrex is the only thing that can combat my pain, so I take 200mg in the morning and at night. As I have told you before, I find anti-depressants an absolute necessity, and I have found Effexor, which has both seretonin and dopamine in it, the very best for me. I take 75mg in the morning, for the most part...unless I need that extra help...usually in the winter months, then I go to 150mg per day. Currently I am taking 4mg of Clonazepam and 50mg of gravol to get to sleep at night. As you may be able to tell my insomnia is a HUGE battle for me. When that doesn't work...well let's just say I'm fu......up for the night!

Just in case you are wondering, yes, my doctor prescribes all of these medications, which brings me to my next point of advice. It is essential that you have a doctor who truly understands your illness and your pain. It is important to be able to talk freely with your doctor and know that they will listen and help you as much as they possibly can. I feel lucky to have found my doctor as she has gone to great lengths for me in my depression, my illness, and my disability. It is her that I must thank for her understanding and empathy as she has helped hold me together.

In my coping strategies, I also see a chiropractor once every three weeks. It was not until I threw my back out that I ever went to one…now I wouldn't miss it for the world. I am amazed at how much this has made a difference in the pain level that I endure. My chiropractor is also very wonderful in knowing Fibromyalgia trigger points which is also a necessity, or so I feel, in finding the right chiropractor for you. A big word of advice here is ICE…use it after each visit…or you may be sorry that you hadn't! I also found out that heat is not a very good thing, for the most part, as it draws more blood to the swollen area. An interesting tip, I thought! Warm baths are good, especially if you use Epsom salt in the water and take a towel, dip it in the water…then wrap it around your neck…so you do not have to scrunch down. Unless you are fortunate enough to have a Jacuzzi…then you are all set. That is also one of my recommendations, but not one that I can afford!

Massage therapy is also something that I highly recommend, as I go for one the day prior to going to the chiropractor and things are much looser to enable a good CRACK! At this point, we are covered through Eric's work, so it does not cost us, but if it weren't for that lucky break…I wouldn't be so easy to 'crack up'…a little humor goes a long way!

As human beings, we have so much pride, yet don't let your pride stop you from getting the things that you need. I was guilty of this for a long while, guess that is the LEO in me!

Instead of getting myself a cane to help me walk on those real bad days, I would actually crawl up and down the stairs…stupidity ruled! I now have a cane that I use when I need to, and every time I use it I realize that I may need it permanently sooner or later. I pray for the later…much later but it is not worth the agony to let my pride stand in the way. I asked my children if it embarrasses them when I use it and all they told me was that I had to do what I needed to do. They love me no matter what way I am. I had to wonder then…who was the parent and who was the child?

One specialist that I saw told me that swimming would be a help for my illness, yet when I tried it, I only found that my back seized up as if it were in vice grips! If you have not tried it, it is certainly worth a try…just taking it slow and easy. That is what I have found so crazy about this illness as it has no clear cut therapies, only trial and error for the specific person.

I've also been told to walk every day. This I try to do as much as possible since the rate that the illness is progressing, sometimes I get scared that if I don't walk…I may never be able to. It does not matter how far…and believe me I do not get far but I walk as fast and far as I can to get some exercise, until the pain is overwhelming…yet that is life for us. We must

Kathy M.

accept it as it is, and that of course, is the hardest part for all of us!

"To draw the line of our endurance of pain is healthy…
Yet setting yourself up too high or too low is dangerous!"

It is imperative that my readers know that in writing this book, I am not coming from the scientific end, only the personal end. I by no means am a scientist or a doctor or a professional of any type, for that matter. Yet, I am a REAL person and a real SUFFERER. In writing this book, it is my hopes that you learn coping skills and a much more meaningful life by learning how to love and accept yourself...for who you are. Having said this, it is crucial for you...the ill...and your loved ones know the facts about your illness so that you can be fully informed on your own symptoms and treatments.

Right now, I would like to turn to some other things that may help you cope through your life. These things or methods of treatment are available and although at this stage in my life, I am not ready to go to these types of therapies...I may in the future.

Actually, one that I am looking into now is acupuncture, as I have heard wonderful things about its outcome. It is expensive, yet, so I have heard, if recommended by a physician, it may be covered. I am looking into that now, through Eric's coverage. Cross my fingers and hope for the best, is all I can do...what else is new?

Natural remedies have also had good reviews, some of which I have tried, with little or no improvement. As a result, I am not trying any at the moment since we all know that these are not cheap. It is my thoughts on the matter, at this time, anyway, that if I am not going to reap the benefits, to me there are none. However, as I have stated before...no one's reaction is the same to anything so if you have not tried this path...you may want to look into it. There are many naturalpaths that are very helpful and understanding. Just make sure that the one you choose is for real. I'll tell you a story of why I say that.

It was a long time ago; not long after I became sick that I went to one of these...nut case is all I can say. I am so glad that I had my mother with me as a witness because I am quite sure no one would have believed me otherwise! First of all, his theory was that everyone should have blue eyes because that is what you are born with. According to him, your eyes only changed color if you were full of toxins! God bless my mother, as she has brown eyes, so she asked him if that would mean that she was full of shit! Of course, he ignored her and went on to have me hold bottles of different natural pills to my solar plex. Then he held my hand, as I made a curled thumb and bent it over my pointer finger, to make a circle. This is the freaky part...he then had me hold these bottles and if he could pry my finger and thumb apart...that meant that I needed that specific natural remedy! Can you imagine? Then he had me stand up as he performed some ritual around the aura of my body, flinging his hands up and down, side to side around my body…as I was facing north…as that was essential to the ritual. As you guessed…I never went back there again, and it took both my mother and I to shake it off. It felt like we had entered the twilight zone for a short time. The strange part is…he has faithful customers. Yes, sometimes life is stranger than fiction…don't you agree?

If you have ever read any natural ways to reduce your symptoms, a very big part of this is what you eat. It has been said recently that wheat is bad for Fibromyalgia, as is potatoes. I have heard many things over the years of my illness that should be cut out of your diet. Personally, I feel that I have had to deal with enough being taken away from my life and me, as I once knew it. At the present time it is my choice not to take this or that out of my diet as nothing represents a cure. This is not to say not to try it, and all of us know that there are certain foods that we just can not eat, due to the toll it will take on our body. Two of these things for me are pizza and bananas as my irritable bowel gets downright angry at those. Juice is also a big no-no for me as it also makes my bowels extremely mad, as I've even heard my stomach growl at me…as it swells to twice its normal size! It is well known that to have good nutrition, green vegetables are a must, yet for me they can be a bust! Are you relating?

Each and every one of us are different both in the way we deal with our eating and in our lives and that is what separates us from one another. My thoughts on the above factors are, for right now…just not for me. As you know just by being, ill we have had to give up so much in our lives. I feel that to give up the things we can have and enjoy, is not only depriving ourselves of living to the best of our ability, but also controlling even more of our choices for our own lives. At this point in my life…I am not willing to give these things up, yet that is not to say what is in my future, or how I will react in the choices I make for myself. The important thing to remember is not to deprive yourself of too much, as that can make you feel even more emotionally and physically trapped. The key to our sickness is to make the choices that will lead to our utmost freedom and well being.

'To control your own choices in your life is living…

Yet to have choices dictated to you is only surviving!'

Turning our focus now to the bigger picture called life, it is my belief that we are not suffering for nothing, nor were we chosen for nothing. Yes, however crazy it sounds, I believe that there is a reason why each and every one of us is sick...but please know this. I do not believe that any one of us asked for it, or did anything intentional to receive our misfortunes!

Wow, you are probably thinking...she has really lost it now...one too many marbles have gone astray! Actually...I have often wondered this myself...yet there is no syndrome to prove it...imagine that!

How many people have told you that you are a strong person? How many people have watched you in amazement as you cope day after day? It has taken me a long time to come to the very realization that I am strong, amazingly so. Yet there is still a part of me that wonders...why me...and screams...enough already! However the deeper part of me sees that I have been chosen by a higher power. It is my desire to persevere and overcome all which is dealt to me. This is the part that ties in with my very soul and answers that awesome question, "Why me?"

Since I was stricken with my illness at the age of eighteen, I was too sick to go to college for Early Childhood Education, as that would have been the direction that I would have chosen to go with my studies. Instead...I became a syndromite, allowed to rest and be ill.

I married at the age of 20...definitely, too young...and became a sick and tired housewife! Those of you that are healthy are also sick and tired...I know...yet in a different way! If you are healthy, you may be sick and tired of doing it, yet if you are sick...you can't even do it! Sometimes I am tormented by the fact my house looks like a tornado just went through it!

As I became a human TV guide, knowing what was on every channel, on every single day...don't worry, we lived in the country so cable was not an issue! I became so very bored...so I began to write. This was something that I had always wanted to do, yet it seemed like one of those dreamer things to do, or so I convinced myself at a very young age. Anyway, I began to write a novel, and although it took me ten years to finish it, I realized this was the gift that God had given to me. It is entirely fictional, and if I may say so myself...it is good! As of yet, it is not published, nor have I even sent it away to be published. Why, you ask? My answer is a simple one...I felt the need to write to others who are ill, like myself...my fellow syndromites!

My desire to touch others and help all of us, "Sickies", to feel better, heal, and understand ourselves...at least to the best of our abilities. I wish for every one who is ill, or who loves someone that is, to know that they are not alone. As we walk side by side, we can help each other...after all, is that not what we are here for? To grow as human beings, to love, to help, and to come together as one!

I have been ill for a long time, yet my acceptance is still difficult; as I wonder if I will ever just be content to be a syndromite. In writing this book, I feel that I am truly helping others, while at the same time helping myself. As in my words to you, I also feel an inner healing happening inside of me. Hey, therapy groups that I won't be kicked out of...see what amazing things I am learning! When you are kicked out of therapy...just write a book!

Besides writing, I feel that for some reason I have been chosen to be ill...as a mom. You may be thinking...well anyone can be a mom, accept for the men...sorry guys! However if I had not been chosen to be ill, I feel that I would probably have returned to work, and in doing so, I feel that I would have missed out on the real miracle of being with my children. They are truly a gift, a blessing of love and innocence, kindness and gentleness. I feel that having them with no choice of returning to work...my children and I have been blessed. I have been blessed by the miracle of motherhood and chosen to raise my angels...my children.

Of course, some days I could scream..."CALGONE, TAKE ME AWAY!" Kids are kids, that is for sure...sometimes sweet...sometimes not...yet always a challenge! My children have taught me a lot about who I am as a person...sick or not! Since I have been ill ever since they have been in this world, they have only ever seen that part of me...the sick and the tired part, yet they have always told me that I am the best mom in the whole world. Definitely not believing that one! Yet by watching them grow as people, I can see that just because I am sick...does not mean that I am not good enough.

If you look at your loved ones...they love you for who you are...and before you even think it, yes...you are good enough for all who love you!

Do you see a different side yet, one that makes you feel special in a unique way? Do you realize that what most people are fighting their whole life for...we already have! We are loved and accepted for who we really are, for in being chosen, we became real...just us. We can't act for other people's love or acceptance...nor can we hide behind a false face, which is masked with a false sense of self.

In a life of sickness, it may feel as if you are always taking; yet you must remember that you are giving as well. In whatever you give back there will be compassion, love and an acceptance of others that others may not have. We have been chosen to have a life of patience, unique to ourselves, but not limited to ourselves.

We will ultimately learn to love and accept our syndromes...as many and as hilarious as they come! We have no choice as we are the chosen...wouldn't you agree?

'To choose a life that suits our desires is easy...

Yet to live a life as a chosen one is a gift and an honor!'

Kathy M.

About the Author

This, I guess would be about me! As I have previously mentioned, I have chronic pain and have had to deal with it since my teenage years. I am 33 years old, have been through a divorce, an affair, and through the years, a lot of abusive situations. I have a wonderful fiancé, Eric, who has given me the son that I never had, to whom I love very much…as if he were my very own.

In my first marriage I had two wonderful daughters, that have not only been empathetic, but understanding. Eric, who is my true love; and I have been through hell and back, and still I can count on him, always…to be there for me in ANY way that I need. My given names are Kathy Marie, and as you could see from reading, my nickname is Kat. I was born in Ottawa, Canada, yet I lived most of my life in Ontario, Canada. I am a grade thirteen graduate with a two-year-old sense of memory.

I pride myself on standing up for myself…sometimes to the point of stubbornness…on being a good mom…a good wife…a good friend…a good person! My strength amazes even me. My love of life shows in every thing I do. I love to laugh, but most of all I love to make others laugh.

I take great pride when I say that my mom is the best, and I admire her strength and kindness throughout her life. I take one day at a time, as best as I can, and I keep smiling. Here is hoping that you keep smiling, too.

See…no one can do it alone, and without God, my heavenly dad, I could not be here today.

So open up your heart, be grateful and peace will come to you as well. Just listen to your inner voice…and you too will be grateful. For I truly believe that He has given me the words and the wisdom to write this very book. Spirituality does not come from a church or even a bible, it comes from your soul…and no one…not even an illness can take that personal relationship away from you. Only growth comes from the power of your spirit…so grow!

Once again, thank you to all my readers, and I hope you close my book, only to open it up from time to time. After all, it can't hurt to read it over once in a while, especially when you are lonely. I want to be there with you always! Besides, with our memory, it will be like reading something new…don't you think? Keep Smiling…xoxo Kat

Printed in the United States
15668LVS00001B/136-162